AWAKEN!
Sonnets for The Modern Person

Stefan Washburn

ISBN 978-1-63784-414-4 (paperback)
ISBN 978-1-63784-415-1 (digital)

Copyright © 2024 by Stefan Washburn

All rights reserved. No part of this publication may be reproduced, distributed, or transmitted in any form or by any means, including photocopying, recording, or other electronic or mechanical methods without the prior written permission of the publisher. For permission requests, solicit the publisher via the address below.

Hawes & Jenkins Publishing
16427 N Scottsdale Road Suite 410
Scottsdale, AZ 85254
www.hawesjenkins.com

Printed in the United States of America

Dedication

For my family, friends, and loved ones. I thank you all for supporting me during the sometimes painful, sometimes blissful, lifelong expansion of my awareness. May these humble lines serve to encourage others on their own path toward self-growth.

Table of Contents

Sequence Nr.	Title	Date
1	Sunday Sonnet	12Aug2018
2	Without Hope of Love	19Aug2018
3	Beauty Brought to Terms	02Sep2018
4	Time's Cruel Advance	12Sep2018
5	I Am Your Heart	03Feb2019
6	From Solitude I Give to You My Words	02Mar2019
7	The Moment Began	07Mar2019
8 (Corona 1)	No More, My Too-Generous Heart	16Apr2019
9 (Corona 2)	To Elevate Love to Prominent Place	19Apr2019
10 (Corona 3)	Mutual Love, Earnestly Sought by Both	02May2019
11 (Corona 4)	We Are Poised: Let Time Fulfill Love's Design	09May2019
12 (Corona 5)	We Cannot Fail to Achieve Parity	12May2019
13 (Corona 6)	Time Will Tell How Well I Have Loved Myself	18May2019
14 (Corona 7)	When at Last Shall I Achieve This: Love's Dream	24May2019

Sequence Nr.	Title	Date
15	It Is a Quite Calm and Quiet Morning	16Jun2019
16	A Father's Pride Could Never Be Greater	25Aug2019
17	Armed with Grace	12Oct2019
18	I Saw Her Come as a Figure of Light	13Oct2019
19	Lo! We Are the Stuff of Which Art is Made!	14Oct2019
20	There Are Two Men	06Dec2019
21	I Hope to Step Away	01Jan2020
22	One's Very Life by Her Own Hand Bereft	27Jan2020
23	Let Me Pour	21Feb2020
24	May We Forward Walk	23Jan2020
25	Visions Come to Me in Dreams	01Mar2020
26	Love That Endures	05Mar2020
27	I Have Lost My Best Prospect	22Feb2020
28	What is the Value of Me	07Mar2020
29	As Humans We Are Such Social Creatures	22Mar2020
30	It is Quite Clear	28Mar2020
31	Something Tells Me I Have Been Here Before	02Apr2020
32	A Simple Day	12Apr2020
33	I Stand as Proxy	18Apr2020
34	Let Us Attend the Fate Our Gods Have Planned	19Apr2020
35	'Tis A Lovely Spring Day	20Apr2020

Sequence Nr.	Title	Date
36	We Find at Times, Indeed, We Have Enough	21Apr2020
37	Ah, Beauty! You Have Ever Been My Grail!	22Apr2020
38	In the Erstwhile Guise of Becoming Whole	23Apr2020
39	To Contend with Wounds that Have Been Laid Bare	24Apr2020
40	I Gave My Heart to Another's Keeping	25Apr2020
41	I Had No Expectation, and No Hope	26Apr2020
42	Life: There Are No Promises Made Therein	27Apr2020
43	Worthy of Love	28Apr2020
44	Come, Love	29Apr2020
45	You Tell Me	30Apr2020
46	Greetings My Friend	01May2020
47	My Furry Friend	02May2020
48	The Storm This Morning	03May2020
49	What A Year	04May2020
50	My Cat	05May2020
51	Concerted Daily Effort	06May2020
52	Oh, I that Am	06May2020
53	Raise Then a Glass	07May2020
54	A Task Accomplished	08May2020
55	Response to Comments Upon Reading One of My Sonnets	09May2020

Sequence Nr.	Title	Date
56	Those Places Most in Need of Our Profoundest Love and Compassion	10May2020
57	The Morning Cup	11May2020
58	When at Last	12May2020
59	Though a Man of Heart	13May2020
60	The Hollow Invitation	14May2020
61	The Goddess Appears	15May2020
62	The Expense of Spirit	16May2020
63	For Edna St. Vincent Millay	17May2020
64	My Doggerel Lines (or Pizza & Beer)	18May2020
65	The Wet Basement	19May2020
66	On Edna St. Vincent Millay's Poetry	20May2020
67	Time in Poet's Reverie	20May2020
68	Tangible on Ineffable Depends	21May2020
69	The Morning Ride	22May2020
70	Treasure These Last Few Days	23May2020
71	Hath She Held Him in all Too High Esteem?	24May2020
72	When I Shall Have Landed	25May2020
73	First Day Back After Five Weeks Furlough	26May2020
74	I Love These Cool Evenings	27May2020
75	Another Evening at Home	28May2020
76	Many Diverse Media	29May2020
77	Call It Grace	30May2020
78	Fortune Favors Fools	31May2020
79	Hard Times Indeed	01Jun2020

Sequence Nr.	Title	Date
80	Our HR Manager – for Leah	02Jun2020
81	Community Is Not Merely a Group	03Jun2020
82	I Shan't Answer	04Jun2020
83	In A Pinch	05Jun2020
84	The Glorious Music of Bach	06Jun2020
85	The Inner Landscape	07Jun2020
86	Frost-white Frozen Man	08Jun2020
87	You Sent Your Heart	09Jun2020
88	Time's Not Love's Fool	10Jun2020
89	All's Well That Ends Well	11Jun2020
90	Do Not Go Down	12Jun2020
91	My Day's Highest Pleasure	13Jun2020
92	Not Take Away	14Jun2020
93	Thoughts On Friendship	15Jun2020
94	Harken Well to the Wren	16Jun2020
95	Measured Against the Flow of Time	17Jun2020
96	I'm A Heavenly Mess	18Jun2020
97	The Engineer Assembles	19Jun2020
98	This Moment Holds	20Jun2020
99	Peaceful People Protest	21Jun2020
100	To Please the Piper	22Jun2020
101	All That I Am	23Jun2020
102	Let Me Circle Back	24Jun2020
103	A Screaming Panic	25Jun2020
104	Joy of Working	26Jun2020
105	Failure's A Risk	27Jun2020

Sequence Nr.	Title	Date
106	I Open Myself	28Jun2020
107	*Graphis scripta*	29Jun2020
108	How Would That Appear	30Jun2020
109	With Spirit Imbued	01Jul2020
110	My Vertigo	02Jul2020
111	Whether or Not	03Jul2020
112	Love Is So Vital	04Jul2020
113	It's None of My Concern	05Jul2020
114	You Are a Portal	06Jul2020
115	He Who Quips Well	07Jul2020
116	These Poems I Have Fashioned	08Jul2020
117	I Am Vulnerable	09Jul2020
118	The Salmon of Knowledge	10Jul2020
119	Ipse Dixit	11Jul2020
120	I Speak My Heart's Message	12Jul2020
121	I Saw the Goddess Once Again	13Jul2020
122	With Selfless Acts	14Jul2020
123	Does Setting Always Promote	15Jul2020
124	It May Well Be	16Jul2020
125	Have I Done Well by Thee	17Jul2020
126	To Honor Deep Love	18Jul2020
127	Let the Tide of Life	19Jul2020
128	Time, It Seems	20Jul2020
129	How is it Grace and Sorrow Coexist?	21Jul2020
130	Umbels of White	22Jul2020
131	Many the Solar Orbits	23Jul2020

Sequence Nr.	Title	Date
132	Ancient Tongues	24Jul2020
133	Eros is Relatedness	25Jul2020
134	Your Gentle Heart	26Jul2020
135	Brother, Speak Now!	27Jul2020
136	My Lobgesang	28Jul2020
137	Hallowed Words – Hallowed Halls	29Jul2020
138	Tell Me that You Love Me	30Jul2020
139	Even If She Does Not Respond	31Jul2020
140	When Night Falls	01Aug2020
141	More Strength Means More to Offer	02Aug2020
142	The Union I Seek	03Aug2020
143	Nothing Is Lost	04Aug2020
144	Man That I Am	05Aug2020
145	You Hold So Much Love	06Aug2020
146	My Heart's Clear Behest	07Aug2020
147	A Body's Animation	08Aug2020
148	Across The Ages	09Aug2020
149	Being A Poet	10Aug2020
150	Courage	11Aug2020
151	I Don't Have to Hold You	12Aug2020
152	I Grow a Little	13Aug2020
153	Our Tears Have Smiles	14Aug2020
154	Open Your Eyes	15Aug2020
155	A Poet's Separation	16Aug2020
156	The Tongues of Man	17Aug2020
157	A Whole Man	18Aug2020

Sequence Nr.	Title	Date
158	Your Love of Family	19Aug2020
159	The Fisherman and the Nereid	20Aug2020
160	In the Black of Night, He Came	21Aug2020
161	Here's to Whatever Fortune	22Aug2020
162	I'll Kiss Your Hand	23Aug2020
163	My Loveliest Art	24Aug2020
164	What Have You Found	25Aug2020
165	I Love You, Exactly	26Aug2020
166	Autumn's Solidago	27Aug2020
167	Life is Accommodating	28Aug2020
168	Linnaeus' Joke	29Aug2020
169	Chambers of the Heart	30Aug2020
170	My Heartfelt Call	31Aug2020
171	My Father Laughed	01Sep2020
172	Play This One Out	02Sep2020
173	Wise Care of the Self	03Sep2020
174	Is Life Precious?	04Sep2020
175	As Each Day Turns	05Sep2020
176	The Adoration in His Eyes	05Sep2020
177	Got Angst?	06Sep2020
178	Leave It Lay	07Sep2020
179	My Heart's Love-Culmination	08Sep2020
180	If You Value Us	09Sep2020
181	To See Love and Beauty	10Sep2020
182	Held in the Witch's Grip	11Sep2020
183	Term Limits for Marriage	12Sep2020

Sequence Nr.	Title	Date
184	Gravel to Your Sand	13Sep2020
185	Love Expressed in Chemical Engineering Terms	14Sep2020
186	No Sign of Strength	15Sep2020
187	*Ego Laudo Te*	16Sep2020
188	Two Halves of Me	17Sep2020
189	Claire's Sonnet	18Sep2020
190	Ignominious Dreams	19Sep2020
191	The Amazing Wonder-Jill	20Sep2020
192	Ruth Bader Ginsburg	21Sep2020
193	Stop Projecting!	22Sep2020
194	Seeing Is Believing, Holding Is Knowing	23Sep2020
195	Love Was No Misstep	24Sep2020
196	The Poet's Prayer	25Sep2020
197	Loneliness is a Poor Midwife	26Sep2020
198	These Extraordinary Times	27Sep2020
199	Social Forbearance	28Sep2020
200	The Dark Side	29Sep2020
201	Was Gibran Wrong?	30Sep2020
202	Folly's Careless Grinning Mask	01Oct2020
203	Steadfast, He Opens His Heart	02Oct2020
204	Open to Those in Need	03Oct2020
205	The Turning Stone Grinds	04Oct2020
206	When Hearts Beat the Same	05Oct2020
207	Justly Honor the Goddess	06Oct2020
208	Healing Has Its Own Momentum	07Oct2020

Sequence Nr.	Title	Date
209	Love, Give Me Your Hand	08Oct2020
210	His Beautiful Heart	09Oct2020
211	Fall Birdwatching	10Oct2020
212	Return to Reverence	11Oct2020
213	The Grand Game Called Love	12Oct2020
214	Dreams Pose the Irrational	13Oct2020
215	No Spirit to Inspire or Ignite	14Oct2020
216	On Seeing Several Trump Campaign Signs in Rural America	15Oct2020
217	Friendship's Hidden Blessings	16Oct2020
218	Friendship's Truths	17Oct2020
219	Euterpe's Apotheosis	18Oct2020
220	Secrets of Good Craft	19Oct2020
221	Soft Now, My Friend	20Oct2020
222	Love is Stronger than Time	21Oct2020
223	A Love We All Might Pursue	22Oct2020
224	Mae, Where Are You Going?	23Oct2020
225	Enough of Egos	24Oct2020
226	A Clear Path	25Oct2020
227	Each Love You Carry	26Oct2020
228	Mankind's Endeavor	27Oct2020
229	No Great Plan	28Oct2020
230	The Rhythm of the Sea	29Oct2020
231	Cool Grey Introspective Days	30Oct2020
232	Adversity's Sweet Uses	31Oct2020
233	Sigils Are Portals	31Oct2020
234	Invitation to Friendship	01Nov2020

Sequence Nr.	Title	Date
235	Chestnut	02Nov2020
236	Scrumptious Soul	03Nov2020
237	Come My Sweet Muse	04Nov2020
238	*Amara Animum Aggravat Adversum Corpus*	05Nov2020
239	The Complex Heart	06Nov2020
240	Too Early to Celebrate, or Bad-President Blues	07Nov2020
241	The World Awaits	08Nov2020
242	Soft Are the Knells	09Nov2020
243	To Love's Advantage	10Nov2020
244	Though I Sit Alone	11Nov2020
245	Dance as Metaphor for Life	12Nov2020
246	Incredible Soul-Ally	13Nov2020
247	Show Some Spine	14Nov2020
248	The Healing Path	15Nov2020
249	Soul-Space	16Nov2020
250	Sweet vs. Erudite	17Nov2020

Sunday Sonnet
(Sonnet I)

A poet's complaint consists of just these:
His condition, your condition, time, death,
Always love: hard enough to steal one's breath,
Soft enough even the proud gods to please.

How shall he relate these variate things,
Objects upon which the poet's mind acts?
Simply as matters of discernéd facts,
Or with rhythm, rhyme for ornaments sings?

Shall he reveal cherished secrets of his heart;
Bring new vantage to familiar scenes
Like new spice to a plate of common beans?
What shall set his verse from others' apart?

Whether by cunning artifice alone,
Or through his expansive vision be known?

Rhyme scheme: ABBA CDDC EFFE GG

Without Hope of Love (Sonnet II)

"Tell me, what are you hiding in your heart?"[1]
Some shadowy she, some lovely Polly?
Some angel face, in your sullen folly,
Whose countenance demands reason depart?

Her radiance surely shines from within,
But its powerful effect on my heart
Is due, no doubt I think, in no small part
To the expectant state my mind is in.

Could I but shed my need for warmth and love,
To rid myself of all my heart's desire,
Sit content with the will of gods above,
Would I forfeit my precious inner fire?

Then what would there be left for me to hope?
If no fulfillment, then no drive to cope!

Rhyme scheme: ABBA CDDC EFEF GG

---

[1] W.H. Auden, The Age of Anxiety

BEAUTY BROUGHT TO TERMS
(SONNET III)

"That beauty should be brought to terms by me:"[2]
This my heart's desire, and perhaps my shame:
To touch, admire, I hope that such could be;
While covet, possess, or own would bring blame.

Love is free, always a gift well-given,
With many benefits distributed.
Once gone, its certain return disputed
By the vast lonely mass of hope-shriven.

Yet the simple power of a deep soul
To inspire and lift up out of darkness,
To encourage growth and bring to fullness:
In this way, love fills the hungry ones' bowl.

May my well-intended contribution
Feed another's most-sought resolution.

Rhyme scheme: ABAB CDDC EFFE GG

---

[2] Edna St. Vincent Millay, "Fatal Interview", Sonnet X

Time's Cruel Advance
(Sonnet IV)

Lo, we cannot stop time's cruel advance,
While the steps we take diminish each day.
We shall be, at last, unable to dance
When our vigor and color turn to gray.

Let us be content, then, with growing old,
Make a proud show of dignity and grace,
Find our true beauty in these years of gold:
With a firm smile our pending deaths to face.

It is the poet's fine and happy task
To seek beauty where others might not look,
To frame what lies behind a stolid mask,
And read the lines inscribed in heaven's book.

This, my gift: of precious images found.
Hold them fast, if all their virtue be sound.

Rhyme scheme: ABAB CDCD EFEF GG

I Am Your Heart
(Sonnet V)

I am your heart, come alive yet again.
Let us journey to your deep and your dark:
In my arms you shall not fear any pain.
My strength and your light shall not miss the mark.

There, we two, shall ignite the sacred flame,
By which the world's true colors are revealed.
Ours shall be the love of history's fame.
Our legacy: the list of those we healed.

So, my love, my soul, accept this my hand.
We'll touch those hearts that come within our reach,
And send back their suffering for remand,
To staunch the world's wounds with care fit for each.

One smile, one hand of friendship, at a time.
Who knows darkness well may shed light sublime.

Rhyme scheme: ABAB CDCD EFEF GG

From Solitude
(Sonnet VI)

From solitude I give to you my words,
In fervent hope that spirit can be shared,
When hearts clean and clear are finally bared,
Not lost to the wind like heaven-bound birds.

Take them, hold them close, so that their content
May at last have its intended impact;
Though twined in harmony with grace and tact,
The message they carry is quite ardent.

Thoughts traversing the depths of time and space,
Missiles of æther and light propagate
Through the great still void unto heaven's gate
Where, host as witness, we present our case:

That life should opportunities afford
To distribute freely from Love's own hoard.

Rhyme scheme: ABBA CDDC EFFE GG

The Moment Began
(Sonnet VII)

The moment began with fervent intent,
Packed full of content, bound with shared consent,
Then lost for mutual interest lacked:
All love forfeit when out of sight she backed.

My thoughtful words, my considerate acts
(I face now these uncomfortable facts)
Failed fully to touch her sensitive heart.
Timing, or my unseen faults, made us part.

Then what can one say or do when love sours
About a friendship that lasted only hours?
Yet still, to those brief shared moments I cling,
Though they shall never joy to my heart bring.

Why can't I let go of the painful past,
Armed with unbound hope face the future vast?

Rhyme scheme: AABB CCDD EEFF GG

No More, My Heart
(Sonnet VIII)

No more, my too-generous heart, no more,
Shall we depend on other souls' bequest,
To make our deepest self-esteem seem blessed,
But into our own core our love shall pour.

"Give not your heart to another's keeping."[3]
This was Gibran's most deep and wise concern,
That we should, to love ourselves, clearly learn.
But can we manage this without weeping?

All our past hopes, dearest dreams, long-since lost,
Flames of love extinguished by Time's sweet reign,
We witness soul's ascent at ego's wane,
Call back to mind purchased-peace's quite dear cost.

So, we bargain not just for today's grace,
But elevate Love to prominent place.

14 Lines, 10-Syllable, ABBA CDDC EFFE GG

---

[3] K. Gibran, "The Prophet", paraphrased

To Elevate Love
(Sonnet IX)

To elevate Love to prominent place
Is but to serve her at every turn,
To make each act, thought, have one concern:
To bring to light Love's deepest inner face.

Let us then distill life's ardors and pains,
Until all that is left is liquor sweet.
We do this when we apply passion's heat,
By giving those in need sustaining gains.

Peace and love aren't held in isolation:
There is no joy had in other's sadness.
In your well-being do I find gladness,
In unity we achieve resolution.

My happiness clearly hangs on shared growth,
Mutual love, earnestly sought by both.

Rhyme scheme: ABBA CDDC EFFE GG

Mutual Love
(Sonnet X)

Mutual love, earnestly sought by both,
As we embrace challenges in our lives,
Our need for connection our union drives,
Though to part with hopes and dreams we are loath.

The antidote to a poisoned spirit,
Is to join in community of souls:
Persons inclined towards similar goals.
Together we may earn respect's merit.

So, with this regard let us join our hands.
Together we can create new ventures,
Build for us all as-yet-undreamed futures,
With people of open hearts from all lands.

For mankind's future with thought and care fine
We are poised: Let Time fulfill Love's design.

Rhyme scheme: ABBA CDDC EFFE GG

We Are Poised
(Sonnet XI)

We are poised: Let Time fulfill Love's design,
While we work to manifest our best dreams
By clearing our egos of clouded steams.
Let Fortune's wheel bring forth a future fine!

We open our hearts to what time presents,
With resolute focus on refined goals.
Our vision anticipates fulfilled souls,
As predictable as the moon's ascents.

In community we can create this,
Rising to the challenge, touching others,
Becoming everyone's sisters, brothers,
Building momentum, we drive toward bliss.

By making Love our first priority
We cannot fail to achieve parity.

Rhyme scheme: ABBA CDDC EFFE GG

WE CANNOT FAIL
(SONNET XII)

We cannot fail to achieve parity,
Balance between our needs and our desires.
So, let us stoke passion's eternal fires,
With simple acts of open charity.

We know that charity begins at home,
Thus, having compassion for our own faults
Leads to knowledge behind others' assaults.
The gems we glean fill a ponderous tome.

I boldly ask myself for forgiveness:
It is my own scrutiny I must pass.
Does my spirit's weight carry enough mass?
Can I withstand this self-sustained witness?

One tries to "love thy neighbor as thyself",
Time will tell how well I have loved my self.

Rhyme scheme: ABBA CDDC EFFE GG

TIME WILL TELL
(SONNET XIII)

Time will tell how well I have loved myself:
If I maintain levity in hardship,
Self-respect seeking companionship,
Or, seeking love, hide my heart on a shelf.

To myself do I pose the greatest risk –
If my behavior is obsequious,
It becomes to me most injurious.
So, dispense with this, my love, and be brisk!

To serve the greater Self requires finesse:
Dealing directly with the unforeseen,
Knowing when 'tis best not to intervene.
Gods, my growth (slow atime it seems), please bless!

I look to the bright day, my eye agleam,
When at last I shall achieve this: Love's Dream.

Rhyme scheme: ABBA CDDC EFFE GG

When At Last
(Sonnet XIV)

When at last shall I achieve this: Love's Dream?
When I am not solely preoccupied
With my own sorry state, so vilified,
Letting go, to enter the hoped-for stream.

When my destiny finds me, will I be
Ready to act as pure Love's conduit?
How to become this I must intuit:
To offer up my heart, unfettered and free!

So, I begin today with sunny heart
And approach the day's events full a-smile
My eye alert to the path ahead, while
Knowing that contentment is my true art.

This growth I have earned, I shall not un-grow:
Adore, my quite generous heart, adore!

Rhyme scheme: ABBA CDDC EFFE GG

It Is A Calm Morning (Sonnet XV)

It is a quite calm and quiet morning.
So, I sit serene, teacup in my hand,
Waiting for what the Gods this day have planned,
Listening to the soft raindrops falling.

Shall I hear voices filled with laughter and joy,
And see another's eyes sparkle with mirth?
Since of these things my current life is dearth,
To manifest them what shall I employ?

How best to create the life we most need,
And become the beacon for good fortune.
By shining forth hope, purchase nature's boon.
To fulfill this challenge, the Gods I plead.

Here's hope that I can say without chagrin:
Bring it on! Let this wonderful day begin!

Rhyme scheme: ABBA CDDC EFFE GG

A Father's Pride
(Sonnet XVI)

A father's pride could never be greater,
Than is mine for you, my dear, precious one.
The qualities you possess, dearly won,
Show wisdom others accrue much later.

Your steadfast devotion to compassion,
Demonstrates heightened social awareness:
For prudent justice a confirmed witness,
Equality pursued with conviction.

Yet my admiration does not depend
On your many personal achievements.
These things don't define you. Just like garments,
They only serve to extend and append.

No, these are not you. Your soul is more vast.
<u>There</u> is the source of beauty, unsurpassed.

Rhyme scheme: ABBA CDDC EFFE GG

Armed with Grace
(Sonnet XVII)

Armed with sensitivity, a sharp mind,
Grace of intention, and ever humor,
My life in full flower is no rumor.
Friede und freud,[4] peace and joy shall I find.

I have found our best heartfelt achievement
To share with those who need: our boundless heart.
Finding ways to help others, this our art.
Thus, with thoughtful care we find fulfillment.

Create then a sense of pervading grace,
Surround oneself in a field of pure bliss.
Our loving efforts shall not go amiss.
So, hold fast to these joys, and them embrace.

Though we cannot correct all injustice,
By our example may we be of service.

Rhyme scheme: ABBA CDDC EFFE GG

---

[4] German: Peace and Joy

I Saw Her Come
(Sonnet XVIII)

I saw her come as a figure of light,
Though she did not see herself in this way:
Her radiance hidden from her own sight.
The ego thus veils the bright soul by day.

She stood thus in the sun, wind at her back,
Receiving all that the day had to offer.
From joys mixed with ashes, she did not slack,
Her will, at peace, with all life might proffer.

Since her own angelic soul far outshone
The many heavy troubles of this world,
Her spirit's ascendency was foreshown:
Unveiled, her magnificence was unfurled.

This strength, most surely from the soul, a boon.
Such wisdom and grace, rare to come so soon.

Rhyme scheme: ABAB CDCD EFEF GG

Lo! We Are the Stuff (Sonnet XIX)

Lo! We are the stuff of which art is Made!
Hold to that and bear life's many foibles,
While Love's promises become tangibles.
Let us then ensure that hope shall not fade.

For this reason, angels of light love us:
We are their especial proud governance,
As they seek our spirit's growth to enhance.
May we do this with little fuss or tuss.

Love and death, our traveling companions,
Shall stay ever with us, so we hold them close,
Lest our dreams should become too grandiose.
Who then should fund our ego's rebellions?

Determined to work toward Future's peace,
We sustain our hope, and our fears release.

Rhymed scheme: ABBA CDDC EFFE GG

There Are Two Men
(Sonnet XX)

There are two men in my one body:
One who feels the dull ache of loneliness,
One who is friends with our separateness,
Yet feels not separate from anybody.

So how may these two selves live together?
How reconcile their quite different needs?
Can one that is free, and one whose heart bleeds,
Learn to accept each other as brother?

This appears to be my standing challenge:
Give weight to the struggle for harmony.
Union of soul is my epiphany,
My best hope for wholeness on this does hinge.

Patience, my love, let time its fullness bring.
Allow the heart its brightest song to sing.

Rhyme scheme: ABBA CDDC EFFE GG

I Hope to Step Away
(Sonnet XXI)

I hope to step away, and leave behind
My erstwhile enthralling fascination,
Hopes, desires: my puerile recreation;
A clearer path toward deeper love to find.

By holding my best self in focus while
Acting for the benefit of others,
I hope to serve my sisters and brothers,
And thereby my greatest strengths to reconcile.

Not to deny my own personal need,
Yet may my work another purpose serve,
That through this would I develop the nerve,
To ensure Love's (not my) designs succeed.

You see, no doubt, my growth at times quite slow,
Never still, but subject to ebb and flow.

Rhyme scheme: ABBA CDDC EFFE GG

One's Very Life
(Sonnet XXII)

One's very life, by her own hand bereft,
Leaving us, her survivors, to ponder:
Oh, what singular hurt, we may wonder,
Hath her dear heart harshly asunder cleft.

Alas that so desperate of an act,
Should eternally upon our soul's tableau,
Inscribe there an unhappy note so low,
We cannot divest our heart of this fact.

Here is my deepest person open laid:
To witness another's despair and pain,
Knowing her choice, (my efforts were in vain,
Even with my love), could not be unmade.

Is the fault ours, and ours alone, to own?
Nay, for mine never was a heart of stone.

Rhyme scheme: ABBA CDDC EFFE GG

LET ME POUR
(SONNET XXIII)

Let me pour thy wine, though my hands tremble.[5]
Belovèd, my love has no hold on thee.
Thou'rt not mine, yet I revere thee greatly.
Nay, I mock not Love by this plain semble.

I walk away, with grace, and empty hands.
I have given all that you would receive.
My heart offered more than we did achieve.
For we keep decorum, as life demands.

Be off to other horizons then, friend.
Fulfill your dreams through some other man's care,
But witness how my gentle heart is bare.
I pray that you find true peace in the end.

With great admiration and deep respect:
May life bring you every good prospect.

Rhyme scheme: ABBA CDDC EFFE GG

---

[5] Elizabeth Barret Browning, Sonnets from the Portuguese, XXIII

May We Forward Walk (Sonnet XXIV)

May we forward walk in soft harmony,
And find between our every step, grace;
Spreading joy with the brightness in our face,
Creating a sweet sort of industry.

Let that be our offering to the Gods,
Whereby supporting all living creatures,
We illuminate Love's many features,
And so, honor those whom our praise lauds.

In such fashion we contribute to Life's
Vital heartbeat, promoting momentum,
Propelling us on to better outcome,
Helping alleviate those daily strifes.

Thus, our deep vision into wonder delves.
What more could we ever ask of ourselves?

Rhyme scheme: ABBA CDDC EFFE GG

Visions Come To Me
(Sonnet XXV)

Visions come to me in dreams, which require
That appropriate response and action
Be taken to the Gods' satisfaction,
Lest I should see some consequence most dire.

Heavenly ones each demand sacrifice.[6]
Humbly we must honor them one and all,
For they reign still strong in our hearts withal.
To deny them, none can afford that price.

To align myself with a higher purpose,
I walk in accord with my dreams' guidance,
Speak with directness, not ambivalence:
Living becomes our life's magnum opus.

That we all may yet live in harmony,
I see as my greatest epiphany.

14 Lines, 10-Syllable, rhymed ABBA, CDDC, EFFE, GG

---

[6] Friederich Hölderlin, "Patmos" – dem Landgrafen von Homburg

Love That Endures (Sonnet XXVI)

Love that endures, from life that disappears![7]
When life loses its sweetest flesh, and more,
To reveal its bright adamantine core,
We find therein honest love without fears.

For only a heart and mind united
Can proffer the strength to endure these pains,
Without regret, accept such modest gains.
And yet, shall we not remain hope-sighted?

Though we stand together, each one must bear
Their own burdens, unfulfilled hopes and dreams.
So, can this, alas, be all that it seems?
What witness can we bring for peace, so dear?

This then, love, just this: love given away
Is not truly gone. No, it's here to stay.

Rhyme scheme: ABBA CDDC EFFE GG

---

[7] Elizabeth Barret Browning, Sonnets from the Portuguese, XLI

I Have Lost My Best Prospect
(Sonnet XXVII)

I have lost my best prospect for real love,
Not mere fancy, but deep love between souls,
One that even the great Goddess condoles.
Some aspects seemed to fit just like a glove.

To this love I gave my best thought and care,
Cultivating harmony of spirit,
Hoping to earn in her eyes equal merit,
To make withal something quite rare.

I do not blame her for this missed attempt.
With me lies the fault of a poor judgement:
Had I possessed a clearer temperament,
From this pain, perhaps, I would be exempt.

It was close, so close, but just not to be.
To love another my heart remains free.

Rhyme scheme: ABBA CDDC EFFE GG

What is the Value of Me
(Sonnet XXVIII)

What is the value of me without you?
What joy may I take in my daily life,
Without the nearness of a longed-for wife?
With no object, does my love still ring true?

With inspiration my heart does open.
Her voice, sparkling eyes, her laughter and tears:
My soul jumps at these signs when she appears.
With the loss of them, shall my life cheapen?

Or shall I lift up my dampened spirit,
Turn love back on myself, and find reasons
To honor my own heart, and its seasons,
Knowing at last my actions had merit?

See, my gifts, now shunned, had markèd impact,
So noble and respectful is but fact.

Rhyme scheme: ABBA, CDDC, EFFE, GG

As Humans We Are
(Sonnet XXIX)

As humans we are such social creatures
A virus causes us to shelter-in-place.
My desire to speak to you face-to-face,
Opposes measures that this time features.

Let us hope that this loneliness bears fruit,
That the time we spend in isolation
Provides benefit to this distraction.
May the seeds we plant here take firm root.

Consider this time as an investment,
Put to good use to develop talents.
While we wait out surcease of pestilents,
Hoping you do not contract this ailment.

So, each of us is called to improvise.
May we grow thereby from this exercise.

Rhyme scheme: ABBA, CDDC, EFFE, GG

It Is Quite Clear
(Sonnet XXX)

It is quite clear to all just how painful
Pandemic-enforced solitude can be.
Our media provides news, certainly,
But to supply true discourse is doubtful.

The heart yearns to reach out and others touch,
To find ways to establish common ground,
So that a field for exchange may be found.
Our egos serve best, just to make it such.

Since for now I cannot look in your eyes,
Nor clasp your dear hand in happy greeting,
Reminds me that precious life, so fleeting,
Is duly enhanced by our love, so wise.

Let us look for new opportunities,
To lift each other, and our hearts appease.

Rhyme scheme: ABBA CDDC EFFE GG

Something Tells Me
(Sonnet XXXI)

Something tells me I have been here before.
When moments of fear I do sometimes face,
When my stomach sinks and my heart does race,
In fear's grip these symptoms come to the fore.

If I give in and succumb to the panic,
Then these problems do seem to overwhelm.
But if I put my wise-soul at the helm,
I surmount issues that seemed titanic.

Letting go of these fears, I seek a path
That offers up tangible solutions,
Such that fears become fascinations.
Ah, see what portents this moment hath!

I can apply this technique, use my strength,
And create fruitful outcomes, to great length.

Rhyme scheme: ABBA CDDC EFFE GG

A Simple Day
(Sonnet XXXII)

A simple day, and what does it offer?
A chance for the renewal of spirit,
If we can hold peace within Time's transit,
Grasping all that this moment may confer.

Thus, through seeking its truest quality,
We may extract each moment's potential,
And attune harmony beneficial,
Bound within a matrix of charity.

For if we achieve this high blissful state,
Is it not incumbent upon us then,
To share this grace with all women and men,
Elevating every one to their best fate?

I hope we find we can answer this call:
To spread community of hope to all.

Rhyme scheme: ABBA CDDC EFFE GG

I Stand As Proxy
(Sonnet XXXIII)

I stand here as a proxy for Love's god,
While you stand in proxy for the Goddess.
May those divine ones our union bless.
Through us they dance, sing, laugh with wink and nod.

Assured by hearts pure, we step out with grace.
I live to see your life's hurdles vaulted.
Through serving you, we are both exalted.
Thus, each day's joys and sorrows we embrace.

I give you my strength of thought and care,
My certainty that all truth will unfold.
We can be seen true by this measure bold:
Free of fears we will fairly forward fare.

Here my friend, I offer my outstretched hand.
Let us attend the fate our gods have planned.

Rhyme scheme: ABBA CDDC EFFE GG

Let Us Attend
(Sonnet XXXIV)

Let us attend the fate our gods have planned!
Reach for the pure stillness of contentment.
Look for opportunities for fulfillment,
And let our noblest passions be thus fanned.

May we find we have the skills requisite
To seek every honest advantage,
To extract each essence of great vintage,
From these elements our lives composite.

Certain this craft can be put to good use,
To make of mundane matters: bright and bold,
Steering by the right star our hearts enfold
In a state of grace both clear and profuse.

To grasp that blissful state, and hold it still,
We find at times we must exert our will.

Rhyme scheme: ABBA CDDC EFFE GG

'Tis A Lovely Spring Day
(Sonnet XXXV)

'Tis a lovely spring day, with birds awing,
Flowers abloom, sweet-scented sunlit air,
Inspired to send our friends wishes fair,
Sharing the many gifts this time does bring.

How grateful I am to have you as friends,
Blessed to witness the love you both do share:
To note how well for each other you care,
For love is best, when tenderness it tends.

Take strength from this time, into your heart deep,
Where your soul may lay claim to worthiness,
Building there in the house of love: fastness
For leaner fortunes to defenses keep.

So, sing today, and dance in joy withal,
A love so rare is admired by all!

Rhyme scheme: ABBA CDDC EFFE GG

WE FIND AT TIMES
(SONNET XXXVI)

We find at times, indeed, we have enough.
Let us therefore take some comfort in this:
We shall survive all that may go amiss,
And live again to smile despite the rough.

We find then we possess resources deep,
Upon which we may call in times of need,
To stillness find, from agitations freed,
By our own efforts, bounty of bliss reap.

Thus, incumbent upon us to manage,
Our responses to both joy and sorrow,
Use this skill with care to greet the morrow,
And will all forbearance its limits gauge.

Like artists, we craft with items at hand,
So, the day's possibilities expand.

Rhyme scheme: ABBA CDDC EFFE GG

Ah, Beauty!
(Sonnet XXXVII)

Ah, Beauty! You have ever been my grail!
How could one ever live without thy grace?
Whether fair of heart and soul, form or face,
Each has its role to play, beyond the pale.

Why would one consider being without
This precious gift, bestowed us from on high?
Life bereft of Beauty would seem very dry,
As a bare streambed in the midst of drought.

Could we still move, without meaning or hope,
And give credence to the demands of the day?
How would we manage to survive that way?
By what means would we even start to cope?

I shudder to think of what might befall,
Without the grace of Beauty on us all.

Rhyme scheme: ABBA CDDC EFFE GG

In the Erstwhile Guise (Sonnet XXXVIII)

In the erstwhile guise of becoming whole,
Seeking union with all that is divine,
While bringing all our parts to aspect fine,
We raise superlative Love as our goal.

Toward this object we fervently drive:
Confused, we elevate the intimate,
To status of most hallowed infinite,
Hoping there our earnest passions shall thrive.

Then how shall this design its intent prove,
If Love be not all,[8] as some have oft said?
Since it's true that on Love our hearts are fed,
Then by simple acts we may mountains move.

Let us then make the most of Divine Love,
With intimacy as its fitting glove.

Rhyme scheme: ABBA CDDC EFFE GG

---

[8] Edna St. Vincent Millay, "Fatal Interview", Sonnet XXX

To Contend With Wounds (Sonnet XXXIX)

To contend with wounds that have been laid bare,
Healing of psychic trauma does require
A spark to ignite the souls' deepest fire,
Refuge of spirit for ritual care.

A harbor safe from storms and gales, where strong
Healing may proceed from within our hearts;
Where we defend ourselves from Fortune's darts;
Learn the skills to oppose all that is wrong.

We can train our thoughts to run on courses true,
Not succumb to unreasonable fear,
Accept our weaknesses as treasures dear:
Parts of life with grace and light to imbue.

These seas seem uncharted in local sense,
But many before us have journeyed hence.

Rhyme scheme: ABBA CDDC EFFE GG

I Gave My Heart
(Sonnet XL)

I gave my heart to another's keeping,
This, alas, despite Gibran's caution wise.[9]
The result, as I'm sure you may surmise,
Was of my own faults' direct reaping.

Some say the soul seeks out experience,
But the folly of youth knows not nurture,
Lacks caution, and respects not its future,
Leading to lessons hard-learned and intense.

One evening I knelt before a woman,
Held out my heart to her: gesture of love.
With quick kick to the chest, she did me shove,
Flat onto my back, now a wiser man!

Be not Love's churl, this or any day,
But have the composure to walk away.

Rhyme scheme: ABBA CDDC EFFE GG

---

[9] Kahlil Gibran, "The Prophet", section on Love

I Had No Expectation
(Sonnet XLI)

I had no expectation, and no hope,
That my love-efforts would be returned,
But of their markèd impact I have learned,
That True Love's designs exceed not my scope.

I give to you all that is in my heart,
And stand here most grateful and resolute,
That my intents shall be without dispute.
By your acceptance I have done my part.

If they are meaningful in some small way,
Fulfilling needs that others may neglect,
In receipt you accord me great respect.
I shall be glad, should they brighten your day.

I beseech the Gods grant to thee thy due,
And pray my acts could help to make this true.

Rhyme scheme: ABBA CDDC EFFE GG

LIFE: THERE ARE NO PROMISES (SONNET XLII)

Life: there are no promises made therein,
But the covenant of the untouched soul,
Free to find its best virtues to extol,
When to drop ego-dreams it may begin.

Self-thwarting contortions of the earth-bound:
Hate, love, sadness, joy, war, peace, health, disease.
Why bear up dualities such as these?
If they aren't helpful why keep them around?

Tell me, what color is the naked truth?
Where is purity beyond the trenches,
If we loose the grip our ego clenches?
When we drop Hope, have we lost all forsooth?

Explain then what creates survival's drive:
Which part carries the strong will to survive?

Rhyme scheme: ABBA CDDC EFFE GG

WORTHY OF LOVE
(SONNET XLIII)

Worthy of love, a woman wished to be.
I first mused: "Well of course, so do we all!"
But what may such a vital need forestall?
What doubt deprives us of security?

We all seek the holy water of Love's grace,
To splash on our brow, and so feel renewed,
To dwell atime with this sweet bliss imbued,
And thus recharged, Life's challenges embrace.

Armed with Hope we may greet each day anew.
Despite all apparent disparities,
We thrive at a banquet of charities.
With providence life shall ever ensue.

To that woman I would give this reply:
"You **are** worthy! Let nothing that deny!"

Rhyme scheme: ABBA CDDC EFFE GG

Come, Love
(Sonnet XLIV)

Come, Love, my heart is open to thee.
Join with me, and see where it will take us.
We share inspiration of high status,
To make each day's essence welcome and free.

Let us find each dark cloud's silver lining,
And through crafting these careful volutions
Perform our spirits' sacred ablutions.
Thus, from Life's deepest ore, be gold mining.

So, let us raise our cup with open smile,
While inconstant Time permits this blessing,
And toast a friendship quite unsurpassing,
That our souls may on this boon sup awhile.

These secrets we seek, yea, have ever sought,
Shall be ours. Our efforts shan't be for naught.

Rhyme scheme: ABBA CDDC EFFE GG

You Tell Me
(Sonnet XLV)

You tell me that you truly like yourself,
Though you admit this was not always so.
I wonder how one becomes one's own foe,
How one may come to denigrate oneself?

From my vantage I see only beauty:
You treat all animals with compassion,
Revealing your heart's deepest affection.
Your actions show strength and integrity.

Your urge to care for those that are quite ill,
From their impending death you don't withdraw,
But pour out all your heart's love, (to my awe)
And bring them some measure of comfort still.

In all my life, I've not seen charity
So freely given, with such clarity.

Rhyme scheme: ABBA CDDC EFFE GG

Greetings My Friend
(Sonnet XLVI)

I send these Beltane wishes your way:
That the days ahead joy and fullness bring
Enough that your beautiful voice will sing.
Accept these blessings on this first day of May.

In Nature may you inspiration find,
With leaf and twig, lichen, and sweet birdsong,
With flowers in bloom, bright stars all night long.
To your soul the bounty of these joys bind.

Then, full of this beauty approach each day,
The blessed work that we have been given,
And through which our survival is driven,
Each of us in our particular way.

So may the joys of this day spirit lend,
To those endeavors which we must attend.

Rhyme scheme: ABBA CDDC EFFE GG

My Furry Friend
(Sonnet XLVII)

My little one meows most fervently.
She follows me around everywhere,
Pleading for me to fill her food-bowl bare.
Trips me underfoot most annoyingly.

I filled your bowl just a short bit ago.
Surely you aren't hungry again so soon?
Why look, it is not yet even noon!
Dinner is at five, you must wait, just so.

Why are you doing this my furry friend?
Your stature denies you are underfed.
Away from here now! Go back to your bed.
Your pestering me is more than I'll tend.

She is cute, and I adore her truly,
Yet she tries my patience twice, thrice, daily.

Rhyme scheme: ABBA CDDC EFFE GG

The Storm This Morning (Sonnet XLVIII)

The storm this morning keeps coming right back.
It woke me early to close the window.
Its intensity does both ebb and flow,
Feigns stillness, then returns with flash and crack!

The Green of Spring, heightened by the dark gloom,
Displayed so well by the storm's great contrast,
Is quite undaunted by this season's blast.
How fearlessly it shows its lovely bloom.

Let us find strength in this example we see:
When we must at times adversity face,
Since contrast enhances beauty, show grace.
Let this, Nature's emblem, our motto be.

To live as well as we are capable,
And reaching out may we others enable.

Rhyme scheme: ABBA CDDC EFFE GG

What A Year
(Sonnet XLIX)

What a year this is, full of surprises.
Who would anticipate self-isolation,
Be kept for an undefined duration,
Losing our good social enterprises.

While face-masks become the height of fashion,
Giving us a plethora of guises:
Evidence of a humor one prizes.
Mankind's farce-comedy brings elation.

So much time spent in the confines of home,
Projects completed as never before.
Yet, we stand inside and look out the door,
With our hearts yearning to step out and roam.

Ah, how simply strange life can be at times:
Even make one write poetry that rhymes!

Rhyme scheme: ABBA BAAB CDDC EE

My Cat
(Sonnet L)

My house is home to myself and a cat.
Though she is by close comparison small
Her large presence fills the house wall-to-wall.
How then shall I not be amazed at that?

She sets the very hour of my rising.
Her will demands I attend to her needs.
Any tardiness performing those deeds,
Results in antics of her devising.

At certain times she is quite full of play:
With tearing about, scattering the rugs,
Clawing furniture, chasing after bugs.
Then she sleeps for large portions of the day.

That my life should be dominated by
One so small, may be cause to wonder why.

Rhyme scheme: ABBA CDDC EFFE GG

Concerted Daily Effort
(Sonnet LI)

I make a concerted daily effort
To examine my soul – write poetry.
This exercise in scribal artistry,
Is paired with insight of a psychic sort.

I'm often confronted with my shadow,
Aspects of self, the ego would deny.
Yet to truly own them I must comply.
To become a whole man is my credo.

How may one integrate these elements,
Make use of them as beneficial gifts,
Such that in proper place the spirit lifts,
To soar above weak and petty judgements?

So, my soul, my love, let us forward wend,
To make space where new talents and old blend.

Rhyme scheme: ABBA CDDC EFFE GG

OH, I THAT AM
(SONNET LII)

Oh, I that am, alas, a lonely man,
And given to dreaming on Love's fair face,
My eye tuned to every woman's grace.
Why must this beating heart see sweet love's ban.

Though I can pour more of my heart into love,
Than most men could ever come close to touch.
Yet my unused skills, go unpraised as much,
Since no hand comes near to fit that glove.

See then, I have no gift of any worth,
If that gift be no good use to anyone.
Perhaps my poetry may reach someone,
And lift a heart from sad despair to mirth.

A noble vocation it would be now:
Convert my sorrow for others' gain somehow.

Rhyme scheme: ABBA CDDC EFFE GG

Raise Then A Glass
(Sonnet LIII)

Raise then a glass of joy to your fine lips.
Look to the bright sun, yet new in the sky.
Find here reasons enough for peace to buy.
Banish those ills that from us our joy strips.

Yesterday's sorrows inform hearts made wise.
Such wisdom, dearly gained, outlines the path
Our feet should tread to sidestep Fortune's wrath:
Step by step welcome destiny devise.

So, learn to rise above human drama.
Follow the guidance flowing from within.
Look to community, find truth therein.
Through sharing, raise our collective karma.

Every step of each person's journey
Marks well the progress of humanity.

Rhyme scheme: ABBA CDDC EFFE GG

A Task Accomplished
(Sonnet LIV)

A task accomplished is a joy in hand.
The greater the time spent in completion,
The greater then the real satisfaction,
If it should appear in some aspect grand.

Working with one's hands to tangible goal,
Cut, fit, stroke by stroke, layer by layer,
Material becomes design's player.
Function, order, beauty, befit the soul.

Challenges by adjustment surmounted,
Imperfections managed with careful skill,
May ultimately give a welcome thrill:
This fine pleasure should not be discounted.

When at last the thing is finally done,
Ah, soon enough another is begun.

Rhyme scheme: ABBA CDDC EFFE GG

Response to Comments upon Reading One of My Sonnets (Sonnet LV)

In sonnets my heart's secrets I have shared,
Baring to all my most personal needs:
Upon thought, word, and soft touch, my heart feeds,
Bound with hope that someday souls may be paired.

At the risk of sermonizing, I spoke
Using the first-person plural pronoun,
That undefined "we", late of great renown,
Though it's my own soul I wish to evoke.

I write to encourage myself, at best.
Were I not introverted, likely then,
I shouldn't write at all (perhaps), but when
My spirit has faced some trial or test.

Thus, I articulate the poetic voice,
In open terms, as is my artful choice.

Rhyme scheme: ABBA CDDC EFFE GG

Those Places in Need of Our Most Profound Love and Compassion (Sonnet LVI)

When at last I achieved enlightenment,
I found grieving and sorrow did not cease,
Nor the urge to resolve conflict, find peace,
Nor the heart-strong search for true contentment.

What changed was just the field of reference,
From the "me"-personal to "we"-global.
Inequities remained quite ignoble.
Yet here I found a place of reverence:

Those things that cause us all deep bitter pain,
Those hurts that travel the whole world over,
Some may have real solutions, moreover,
When we help others it's our fortune's gain.

So, with these enlightened eyes what do I see?
Firstly that I offer my heart to thee.

Rhyme scheme: ABBA CDDC EFFE GG

The Morning Cup
(Sonnet LVII)

The morning cup that pleases the senses,
Ah, how I dearly look forward to thee!
Oh yes, that first cup tastes so good to me,
While the deep blank fog of sleep, it cleanses.

I raise my cup to my lips in your praise.
Your sweet aroma belies your bitter
Taste, yet in truth there is nothing fitter,
To jump-start the beginning of our days.

Some debate whether or not it is best
To sweeten, lighten, or to take it black.
I say: whatever causes the lips to smack,
Leave silliness of debates to the rest.

Give thanks for this welcome drink from the Gods,
And have another then, if the head nods.

Rhyme scheme: ABBA CDDC EFFE GG

When At Last
(Sonnet LVIII)

When at last, I shall again see your face,
It will bring a welcome joy to my heart,
For what are we when fate keeps us apart?
With no friends, we have nothing to embrace.

I possess many fine talents and arts,
Yet they depend on social context for
Display of their inherent worth. Therefore,
I hope you hear what this message imparts.

Whether expressed in words of rhyme, or by
Handshake, loving glance, a generous hug,
A sweet smile, or gifts that our heartstrings tug:
That we need each other I can't deny.

While we have this opportunity let's share
That which is most important: hearts that care.

Rhyme scheme: ABBA CDDC EFFE GG

Though a Man of Heart
(Sonnet LIX)

Though a man of heart, yet am I sinking.
I lack someone to share love's devotions,
A partner to explore our thoughts, notions.
My life needs someone for balance, meaning.

I feel that "measured" love benefits none:
What lacks commitment holds little value,
Without engaged presence a poor venue,
A travesty that's better left undone.

I sense not all slights can be prevented,
While both our egos are forced to expand,
Stretched, strained, re-sized as wisdom will demand.
With this slow growth we must be contented.

To what may we equitably aspire,
When souls ascend above the ego's mire?

Rhyme scheme: ABBA CDDC EFFE GG

The Hollow Invitation
(Sonnet LX)

Her invitation, alas, was hollow.
She had no intention of following through,
Would not make any commitment to you.
It took far too long to see her shadow.

By my desire, my hope, was I made blind.
The scales have at last fallen from my eyes,
Yet I am no happier man, just wise.
Let's hope the next turn better prospects find.

I will always respond to beauty so,
It's not something I could ever alter,
Though to call it Love, I should now falter.
Such delusions I hope hence to forego.

If I could just learn to see with my heart[10]
Perhaps then it wouldn't be torn apart.

Rhyme scheme: ABBA CDDC EFFE GG

---

[10] Antoine de Saint-Exupéry, "Le Petit Prince"

The Goddess Appears (Sonnet LXI)

The Goddess sometimes appears in my dreams,
As silent as a statue on her throne,
Her presence confirms I am not alone.
In awe, I watch as her radiance streams.

That she speaks not tells me much work remains:
Though my ego deserves no accolades,
Through my earnest prayers her grace pervades,
Step-by-step, day-by-day, my growth obtains.

Through my lines I reach out. Do you not hear?
I open my heart, reveal my strivings,
Show how you may set aside misgivings
And so, to your heart your own strengths draw near.

Since for both our health's sake I'm bound to try,
So, as you will ascend, then so may I.

Rhyme scheme: ABBA CDDC EFFE GG

The Expense of Spirit (Sonnet LXII)

The expense of spirit in a waste of shame,[11]
While chasing pretty flames and fancies free,
Pining for a love that would never be.
Ah! There is no one but myself to blame.

I am the crafter of my destiny,
When I look only through these loving eyes
The total person I fail to apprise,
I create my sorrows most willingly.

My too-generous heart I must protect,
Wiser council than loneliness keep,
When seeking connections both fine and deep:
Take time on our qualities to reflect.

In this manner mature wisdom and skill,
Shall apply while exercising my will.

Rhyme scheme: ABBA CDDC EFFE GG

---

[11] William Shakespeare, Sonnet CXXIX

For Edna St. Vincent Millay
(Sonnet LXIII)

The voice of the poetess spoke dark words
Of loves, of all the men she had ever known,
Who took with them their love, now long since flown,
Words still full of passion years afterwards.

With great skill she raised images, long dead,
Of souls' careful and careless gleanings,
Coveted union's many moist meanings,
Images that intrigue, leading heart, head.

With gentle hand she touched her vibrant heart,
Revealing her deepest, most trusted pains,
Sharing visions distilled of Heaven's rains:
Souls' earnest yearnings, by Gods kept apart.

The truths she has spoken are like fine wine:
Rich palette, with subtle hints of divine.

Rhyme scheme: ABBA CDDC EFFE GG

My Doggerel Lines, or Pizza & Beer (Sonnet LXIV)

The time I have spent my doggerel lines
Contriving, may have found better employ
Bringing forth wit for others to enjoy,
For who cares to witness a poet's whines?

Instead of loves long lost, or sadly missed,
Why not a raucous song of joy and mirth?
Why labor long to give painful love birth,
When we could sing of times we all got pissed?

Or that time we gladly entered the fray:
"For Pizza and Friday night!" we shouted.
Alas, in our stupor we were routed,
Yet we lived to laugh it off the next day!

The poet fills many functions, you see,
Not the least of which is to bring us glee!

Rhyme scheme: ABBA CDDC EFFE GG

The Wet Basement
(Sonnet LXV)

Too wet we are, when so much rain descends,
When basements flood, and precious goods invade.
To retrieve them through a pool we must wade,
Their rescue on wet endeavor depends.

As waters recede begins our laments:
Sodden books, old photos and documents
However dear, must now discarded be.
Clothes and fabrics may be washed, thankfully.

The labor of friends helps to recover,
A small portion of forfeit dignity,
From combined-sewers wet ignominy.
By trials our true friends we discover.

When the District's trucks came it was too late.
The waters were gone, not their soggy fate.

Rhyme scheme: ABBA CCDD EFFE GG

ON EDNA ST. VINCENT MILLAY'S POETRY (SONNET LXVI)

Her words, not constrained by standard morés,
Yet of keenly felt beauty, well-apprised
Of our separateness, lines well-devised
To plumb the depths of love in versed forays.

Through skillfully-crafted and well-honed lines
She revealed a vision of love both true,
And painfully honest. A poet's view,
That the poet's own unique scope defines.

Her gift of verse kisses my very soul,
Fitting my mind's eye like glove to a hand.
Who may her open heart's appeal withstand?
Time's æther tempers no urge to console.

Since it is obvious she has touched me,
Does Newton's third law[12] provide equity?

Rhyme scheme: ABBA CDDC EFFE GG

---

[12] Newton's Third Law of Motion: for every action (force) in nature there is an equal and opposite reaction. If object A exerts a force on object B, then object B also exerts an equal and opposite force on object A.

Time in Poet's Reverie (Sonnet LXVII)

The time I spend in poet's reverie,
More valuable this to me than gold,
Here may I let my deepest soul unfold,
Begin to shine my best hope's ministry.

Not just to touch, share time and space, mind you,
But to witness our hearts' transformation,
For truly that is Love's affirmation:
Not what we take, but who we become too.

So will you begin, open now Love's door,
To find who we will be at last, thereby?
We're each other's catalysts, don't deny,
Yet we are both changed in breadth, to the core.

I have thrown the gauntlet, stand here to see,
If you will retrieve, pay the tilting fee.

Rhyme scheme: ABBA CDDC EFFE GG

Tangible On Ineffable Depends
(Sonnet LXVIII)

Tangible on ineffable depends.
Our daily motions do our dreams contain.
Quietly our hearts sing constant refrain,
And to each moment sweet footnote appends.

Some may say self-love; others call it grace.
Does it arise from within or without?
Is there a difference? No, this I doubt.
How do we give evidence, fair to trace?

Many things are known by effects alone.
For who is there has ever seen the wind?
Yet rustling leaves, sails have we examined.
These and many others we have seen blown.

So, within our lives moves a driving force,
Though we see only its effects, of course.

Rhyme scheme: ABBA CDDC EFFE GG

The Morning Ride
(Sonnet LXIX)

With doubtful anticipation I dress
In costume appropriate to the task.
Yet afterwards, I know that I shall bask
In the glow of achievement, nonetheless.

My doubt beforehand is of the hard chore:
The steep grades that must be climbed I misprise,
Though I feel fine during the exercise.
Each day builds on days that have come before.

I've climbed this hill many times afore.
In lowest gear kept spinning, I breathe deep,
Counting each breath, ascend the hill so steep.
Surmounted! Ah, let's do it one time more.

There! I've finished my outdoor velodrome,
So, at last I turn around, head for home.

Rhyme scheme: ABBA CDDC EFFE GG

Treasure These Last Few Days (Sonnet LXX)

Treasure these last few days of pure freedom,
With no demands at all upon my time,
Free to spend luscious hours devising rhyme,
Or not, should other keen interests come.

For next week I return to work at last,
Yet still, in solitude to work from home.
'Tis a sad prospect when feet wish to roam.
I fain would rather be tied to the mast,
And hear the sirens most enticing wail,
That music so rich and sweet, high cabal
To lure the intrepid. Alas, I shall,
Sit alone in this little house, my jail.

So here I will still remain, with only
My cat and dreams to keep me company.

Rhyme scheme: ABBA CDDC EFFE GG

Hath She Held Him in All Too High Esteem? (Sonnet LXXI)

I judge by your quite generous response,
That my verses may reach a space within you.
We may find some accord of fine purview:
Care within courteous conduct ensconce.

Finding grounds for harmonious exchange,
Is my driving impulse. Yet be careful,
Not to grant me status high and doubtful,
Outside of our furthest practical range.

To hold you or I, in too high esteem,
Is dangerous to ourselves and friendship.
To inspire with respect makes strong kinship.
Growth of our wisdom will remain my dream.

This, my friend, is my greatest hope for thee –
I support your strides to be whole and free.

Rhyme scheme: ABBA CDDC EFFE GG

When I Shall Have Landed (Sonnet LXXII)

When I shall have landed on long-sought shores,
My adventural journeys being quelled,
Having faced trials, and dangers expelled,
Retrieved the stone, and done the hero's chores,

Then I shall share with you the sweet nectar
Obtained by these endeavors of mine,
That gossamer of thought, careful and fine,
Born in a suspension of Love's vector,

The blood of æthers whose vibrations ring
With the music of the spheres heard by few,
As beads of light caught in the morning dew.
These wondrous gifts I shall to you then bring.

Until that day, my friend, when my journeys end,
I shall give all I have to Love extend.

Rhyme scheme: ABBA CDDC EFFE GG

First Day Back After Five Weeks Furlough (Sonnet LXXIII)

Well, I have just survived my first day back.
I wouldn't say that I missed the work as
Much as feeling so very busy. Has
This illusion served? Yes, I've got the knack
For providing value added with my time
Spent in consultation with good clients.
Showing regulatory compliance,
Environmental health is ever prime.

A satisfied client often returns
For more assistance at a later date:
Our bosses most-hoped-for lucrative fate,
They're happy when our team revenue earns.

Satisfy the client, and thus our boss.
So, we separate the gold from the dross.

Rhyme scheme: ABBA CDDC EFFE GG

I Love These Cool Evenings
(Sonnet LXXIV)

I love these cool evenings here at home,
Pieces of quiet, interspersed with song,
Floating over the lawns and gardens long
Sailing on past the winking painted gnome.

The front-yard Robin trills its song loudly,
While a distant Wood Thrush echoes clearly,
A Northern Flicker chortles laughingly,
A Mourning Dove coos its sorrow softly.

My favorite Wren's cheerful voice claims all.
None may match its quite exuberant zeal,
With ringing notes in harmonious peal.
Incredibly it shares its joy with all.

Oh, it may rain a little later on,
When all my friends are safely to bed gone.

Rhyme scheme: ABBA CDDC EFFE GG

Another Evening At Home (Sonnet LXXV)

Ah, another evening home alone. Shall
I watch an episode of Star-something
To waste time, or read a book for a fling!
Maybe attend a nearby bacchanal?

(Not that I've ever been to one of course.)
I don't believe the Great God Pan is dead.
Having observed mankind, don't be misled,
He feeds amorous intentions perforce.

Ah, but what of that? Shall the pixies
Tell our covert thoughts to the woodland Queen,
Hidden in her bower of leafy green?
Come little ones! Don't play us these trickseys!

The Queen certain has matters to attend:
If no donkey brays,[13] then all will well end[14].

Rhyme scheme: ABBA CDDC EFFE GG

---

[13] Oblique reference to Titania: Shakespeare, "A Midsummer Night's Dream"
[14] Reference to: Shakespeare, "All's Well That Ends Well"

Many Diverse Media
(Sonnet LXXVI)

Through media of many diverse kinds,
We may declaim feeling or complex thought,
To share news of loves found, horizons bought,
So, all women and men will speak their minds.

I enjoy the written word for nuance,
Which craft of composition helps convey,
All the meanings one wishes to purvey,
Atimes imbued with subtleties, perchance.

Of all communing forms one may survey,
There is nothing quite like a quick side-glance
To jump-start a lonely man's heart (oy vey!),
Though an accompanying smile would enhance.

By music, gesture, dance, and all the arts,
Mankind's languages harmony imparts.

Rhyme scheme: ABBA CDDC CDCD EE

Call It Grace
(Sonnet LXXVII)

Call it grace, bliss, or whatever you will,
By our own hands, be it made manifest.
By our choice of attitude, we do invest
Each moment with cares, and intents instill.

To treat ourselves with respect, love, and care,
Even if others will not grant the same,
In this fashion we may offer no blame,
Finding places our hearts' wisdom to share.

Some parts of destiny we may yet mold,
If thought and actions, we could but control.
Sometime others' help we just might enroll,
In creating harmony, be so bold.

Listen then to what wisdom the heart hath:
Let go the reins, and hold fast to the path.

Rhyme scheme: ABBA CDDC EFFE GG

Fortune Favors Fools
(Sonnet LXXVIII)

Many have supposed: Fortune favors fools![15]
Therefore, then to incur Fortune's favor
Should we, to act most foolish, endeavor?
Yea! Oh, my friends, be not humorless mules.

Let us adorn our heads with Cap-and-Bells!
Let the world know our jovial extents,
Showing all our minds' mirthful contents.
While Humor prevails, it Sorrow expels.

The wisdom of well-considered folly,
Reveals itself as Reason's antidote,
A virtue it becomes us to promote.
Let us therefore laugh long, and be jolly.

For who, pray tell me, could ever deny:
The body prefers to laugh than to cry.

Rhyme scheme: ABBA CDDC EFFE GG

---

[15] Latin: Fortuna favet fatuis

Hard Times Indeed
(Sonnet LXXIX)

These are indeed hard times throughout the land.
George Floyd was murdered by police last week.
For Blacks it's just not enough to be meek.
When hate's the national creed, who may stand
For true justice? Where turn to brothers seek
When care is ministered by back of hand?
Peaceful persons protest to peace demand,
Shot by complete fools in a heartless pique,

Whose manliness is bound to guns they bear.
No courage be witnessed in such weak minds.
Little chance to see hope when anger blinds.
They cannot build who only rend and tear.

What can come out of this utter darkness?
Where's the light to guide us out of this mess?

Rhyme scheme: ABBA BAAB CDDC EE

Our HR Manager - for Leah
(Sonnet LXXX)

Today we lost our HR-Manager.
It was quite a sudden execution,
No time even for Last-Words ablution.
Is this of coming dooms a presage?

There was no chance to share with her our thanks,
For years of service looking out for us,
Or extend our sorrow for her grief. Thus,
Finance over other concerns outranks.

The emotional impact of this loss
On those who stay, with no interceders,
Is seldom considered by our leaders:
With dollars in their eyes, feelings are dross.

This, from a supposed people-culture!
Is our mascot the phoenix, or vulture?

Rhyme scheme: ABBA CDDC EFFE GG

Community Is Not Merely a Group (Sonnet LXXXI)

Where is lasting peace found, but in my hand?
I feel the flow of life from open heart,
As I reach out to you. We're not apart,
Together shoulder-to-shoulder we stand.

Relatedness has its own reserved land.
Step into this space, meet here our own guides.
Hear gratefully what each one confides.
Learn how far our radius may expand.

No energy transfers outside plexus.
Radiance through ether measures as flux:
Implied connection I feel is the crux,
Moving from simple-we to complex-us.

Community's not a collection of bits,
But the pitch intervals between our wits.

Rhyme scheme: ABBA CDDC EFFE GG

I Shan't Answer (Sonnet LXXXII)

Call me by any name, I shan't answer,
Unless it be you call me Love, my dear.
Oh, a gentle response you may well hear:
That would be this body's mind-enhancer,

Not the soul which I duly claim to be.
To dialogue therewith, pay first the fee,
A small tithing to pass the pillared-gate,
So trivial a key to unlock fate.

This outer shell is nothing. Pass me by
Then, if, alas, you can see nothing more,
But if with your Heart's-Eye you see my core,
Open this door, we'll be transformed thereby.

All the world's merely a stage[16] for our dreams,
With hope in hand, we shall honor their themes.

Rhyme scheme: ABBA CCDD EFFE GG

---

[16] Shakespeare, "As You Like It", II:vii

In A Pinch
(Sonnet LXXXIII)

In a pinch, you can be sure of one thing:
I'll not back away from what I have said.
Those overtures that flow from heart to head,
Of these virtues my soul wishes to sing.

Think you this talk of love is wasted air?
Stop for a moment, to examine just
What it really means to you. If you trust,
Then its value against reason compare.

Love is not weak. It is the prime mover,
Permeating all corners of time-space.
For impetus, nothing may take its place,
While our lives we adjust and maneuver.

The path of softness is strongest of all.
I hold to this light, so let kingdoms fall.

Rhyme scheme: ABBA CDDC EFFE GG

The Glorious Music of Bach
(Sonnet LXXXIV)

The glorious music of J.S. Bach,
Is surely mankind's ultimate apex,
Of æsthetic taste and tempered balance,
Whether heard in parts duplex or triplex,
Making him our musical patriarch.
Who else made music Spirit's conveyance?

Be it in Suite, Concerto, or Sonata,
Through compelling and heart-felt melody,
Coupled with high fugal complexity,
Or solo voice, chorus in Cantata,
Exemplifying purest harmony.
In a state of awesome perplexity

The mortal listener's senses are
Gratified, while their soul is uplifted,
From the very first to the final bar.
In having them, truly, we were gifted.

Rhyme scheme: ABCBAC, DEFDEF GHGH

The Inner Landscape
(Sonnet LXXXV)

The inner landscape has quite changed for me,
Being no longer dominated by
Desire for a partner. You might ask why.
Devoting time to writing poetry,
Has stimulated some psychic movement,
Giving rise to a greater sense of self,
And the limiting borders of "myself"
In concert with loneliness abatement.

'Tis enough! This resulting clarity,
Has displaced my daunting desperation.
I seek now for high qualification,
And won't accept less than equality.

The need still exists in my heart for love,
Whether from within, without, or above.

Rhyme scheme: ABBA CDDC EFFE GG

Frost-white Frozen Man (Sonnet LXXXVI)

Frost-white frozen man from another age,
Shamanic symbols covering your skin,
Awaken Shaman! Tell the tales wherein
Spirit is seen to attend the wise sage.

Share your symbols' powerful meanings.
Teach the path of eyes-opened, ears-unstopped.
The weeds of time at last be shorn and cropped,
The ancient temple swept clear for gleanings

Of the dwelling god, whose drums need beating,
Lamps need re-lighting. Teach the hymns to chant,
Reveal the long-forgotten truths extant,
So, assist in this re-birth completing.

Awaken holy one! Herald at last,
News of Hope, to which we have held so fast.

Rhyme scheme: ABBA CDDC EFFE GG

You Sent Your Heart
(Sonnet LXXXVII)

You sent your heart to me in a sealed box,
Closely wrapped in ribbon-tied silk tissues,
From whence all your quite profound love issues.
I pondered a gift so heterodox.

Till I saw it was not your heart but mine,
You had kept and used as it were your own,
For loving notions to refine and hone,
Then to share on wings translucent and fine.

Long the stretches they needed to traverse,
To reach the tuned hearts of those intended;
By combined strength of both our hearts blended,
Signals echoed across the universe.

I placed my heart neatly back in my chest,
Right next to yours, there, in my heart-space nest.

Rhyme scheme: ABBA CDDC EFFE GG

Time's Not Love's Fool
(Sonnet LXXXVIII)

Time is not Love's Fool:[17] Love's folly wastes Time.
Applying for Heaven's gifts to rain down.
Is a fool's cap the lover's earthly crown?
Or is there just cause to keep Love sublime?

Time exists enough for a prudent love,
When all is considered, well-placed and clean,
There is no rush to make it course or mean,
When all right/meet cares have been spoken of.

If Love follows not the heart's yearning,
Desires may require better refinement,
To balance ego in self's attainment,
Where Love's service obtains rightful earning.

Serving Love's aim, through selfless devotion,
Becomes the high Self's love-dance in motion.

Rhyme scheme: ABBA CDDC EFFE GG

---

[17] Wm. Shakespeare, Sonnet 116 – reversed

All's Well That Ends Well
(Sonnet LXXXIX)

All's well that ends well![18] So says Wm Shakespeare,
Our epic bard, whose given name was Bill.
He knew well to guide a plot for max thrill,
Though judged by some back then less than his peer.

Yet admired today most as a model
Of masterful language, whose lines are oft
For a turn of phrase, praised and held aloft;
By writers regarded as an idol.

For double entendre, and bawdy wit,
His plays were quite popular with the folk.
At great conceit and hubris, he would joke,
To bring down arrogance, give cads a fit.

Through his regard for humanity, we can
All agree: what a piece of work is man![19]

Rhyme scheme: ABBA CDDC EFFE GG

---

[18] Shakespeare, "All's Well That Ends Well"
[19] Shakespeare, "Hamlet" II, ii

Do Not Go Down
(Sonnet XC)

Do not go down, sir, into that wild place.
There you will find no great lasting comfort,
No love, forsooth, despite your effort,
No way to keep dignity, or save face.

We have seen her actions often enough,
To be wary of her clear siren's call.
Forget not how you lost your will, and all
Protection against her next sharp rebuff.

When next you give your heart to some woman,
Make sure she has ascended the tower
Of her own highest wisdom and power,
Her eyes open to your coming omen.

Have patience, my friend, all is not yet lost.
Time, it seems, is a strong love's precious cost.

Rhyme scheme: ABBA CDDC EFFE GG

My Day's Highest Pleasure
(Sonnet XCI)

My day's highest pleasure is time well-spent,
In pouring my soul into written verse,
Wherein I devise lines concise and terse,
To complement my thoughts of noble bent.

An exercise which my talent befits,
Requiring consistent even labor
To birth phrases of sufficient ardor,
Which exposition of ideals permits.

My call for love, community, and peace
Among all of mankind's many races,
May Hope bring smiles to all peoples' faces,
And someday, to conflict, a final cease.

Verse is my vehicle for contriving,
Our mutual well-being and thriving.

Rhyme scheme: ABBA CDDC EFFE GG

Not Take Away
(Sonnet XCII)

I am not here to take away your heart,
Nor any precious part of your soul, my dear.
Rather, I shall lead you away from fear,
To Elysian joy, which Love doth impart.

Regard for divine Self must first take hold.
Find that spark within you, to become more
Than ego admits is possible. For
Soon we are bound towards horizons bold.

I see you possess profound empathy
For others. Now turn that great gift around:
Wise care of the self may simply astound,
Helping you find souls of shared sympathy.

With each such move we shall develop grace,
And in our hearts, for Love, find secure place.

Rhyme scheme: ABBA CDDC EFFE GG

Thoughts On Friendship
(Sonnet XCIII)

Here I sit, with my thoughts for company,
To ponder love, life, and relationship,
Shared between friends, treasured companionship:
Valued more when hearts beat in synchrony.

Thus, I seek filial moments of bliss,
When one anticipates the other's moves.
While harmony manifests, joy improves:
Spontaneous laughter goes not amiss.

The bond so forged weaves between kindred souls,
Which through hidden aspects will strengthen both,
Promoting in each, beneficial growth:
Together we march to separate goals.

Friendship provides so many fine delights,
Answer quick its call, when it so invites!

Rhyme scheme: ABBA CDDC EFFE GG

Harken Well to the Wren (Sonnet XCIV)

Harken well, to the mighty morning wren,
Whose zealous joy bursts bright upon the day,
Teaching us all, by example, the way
To approach life, like a master of Zen.

Such profound spirit, in such modest frame,
Undaunted by chill or inclemency,
Shares his opinion of complacency!
With high regard for life his notes proclaim,

That this day is a good one, to be sure,
That all should honor today's precious gift.
Mark well, how a clear song may simply lift,
To each moment add the spice of allure.

Take this special message, and hold it high,
As loudly sings the wren, then so do I.

Rhyme scheme: ABBA CDDC EFFE GG

Measured Against the Flow of Time (Sonnet XCV)

We are measured against the flow of time,
As each day we set that day's goals and tasks,
Dispensing effort as each moment asks.
The care we devote makes each day sublime.

Armed with the calendar and the checklist,
Mankind has built great civilizations,
And seen all the world through explorations,
Yet can't seem to fairly share, and coexist.

The "Us-versus-Them" tribal mindset halts
Any effort made towards global peace.
Till all people are lifted we'll see no cease
Of sorrow or injustice. These our faults!

By our thoughts we create inequity,
With effort we'll create equality.

Rhyme scheme: ABBA CDDC EFFE GG

I'm A Heavenly Mess (Sonnet XCVI)

I'm a heavenly mess sometimes. I know,
It's a good thing that I am so charming,
Or else my presence might be alarming.
See, at least I can make the laughter flow.

At times I dribble soup on my clean shirt,
Or trip in the kitchen over the cat,
Or drop the stirring spoon, but what of that!
So now I wear a bib, and stay alert.

These and my other faults are most dear to me.
They are places to bring my wit to bear:
I can well afford the Fool's Cap to wear.
To laugh at oneself is to be quite free.

So, stay your disdain, let me make it plain,
I shall explain: from mirth do not abstain!

Rhyme scheme: ABBA CDDC EFFE GG

The Engineer Assembles (Sonnet XCVII)

The engineer assembles the data
From many sources and deftly joins them
Into an often-clever amalgam,
Rescues hope from *terra incognita*.[20]

Armed with a pocketful of equations,
Unknowns filled from obscure references,
Carefully plots results to convergence,
Illustrating Design's best summations.

From variable to final outcome,
The process of creation must follow
An aesthetic (of logic not hollow),
Through objective balance to sum, quite plum!

This effort, then, is like music or dance:
When done well, it has power to entrance.

Rhyme scheme: ABBA CDDC EFFE GG

---

[20] Latin: unknown lands

This Moment Holds
(Sonnet XCVIII)

This moment holds the seed of all we are:
We give witness to Time's constant display,
Every instant of every day,
Locked in step with each atom in each star.

Schrödinger suggests we are integral
To the universe's unfolding pattern:
Our movements have unseen impacts in turn
Throughout each corner of time-space-astral.

Quantum paring is a fitting model
Then of our universal connectedness,
Though not new, true in its explicitness,
As all returns to join in a rondel.

I've learned we and the grand cosmos are one.
If true, then at death we are not quite gone.

Rhyme scheme: ABBA CDDC EFFE GG

Peaceful People Protest (Sonnet XCIX)

Peaceful people protest, proposing peace,
Through thorough thinking thereof the throng thrives.
Denouncing decent demonstrations deprives
Celebration ceremonies. So, cease!

Vanity violates valid valor,
Prejudiced posts provide putrid pallor.
Peace-protests protect public principles,
Many manifest mid-municipals.

Hard hatred halts high-minded hand-holding.
Cruel crowd's callous cat-calls cause concern.
Terse taunts turn terrorized tribe taciturn.
World warns: won't win with wisdom-withholding!

Sharing shall show shallow-shameless chagrin –
Daringly defend Democracy's doctrine!

Rhyme scheme: ABBA CCDD EFFE GG

TO PLEASE THE PIPER (SONNET C)

To please the Piper at the Gates of Dawn[21]
We dance in our dreams, dance till we waken,
To those notes our sleeping spirits harken,
To quickly caper with the early faun.

A nymph laughingly cuts across the lawn.
She begs you join in her frivolous dance.
Will you deny the spree, or take the chance?
Act now! Or else awaken with a yawn.

Sleep the restless sleep of erstwhile lovers,
Who are tossed about on the seas of whim,
Like puppets on the strings of seraphim.
Oh, wake not soon, stay beneath the covers!

In love with Love, I do love all the world,
And commit to stand firm as Love's herald.

Rhyme scheme: ABBA ACCA DEED FF

---

[21] Kenneth Grahame, "The Wind in the Willows"

All That I Am
(Sonnet CI)

All that I am, all that I hope to be,
In my remaining journey through space/time,
Is a game of chance, both sweet and sublime,
But what will unfold I cannot foresee.

Life's equation has random elements,
Moments maybe bound to a higher math,
Which must follow a non-linear path,
Derivatives not seen in our figments.

Yet in these outliers, magic resides:
Vectors that give new direction to life,
With hints of unseen force such points are rife.
In opening to new dimensions hope abides,

Hope that momentum will still be conserved,
Such that perfect solutions will be served.

Rhymed ABBA CDDC EFFE GG

Let Me Circle Back
(Sonnet CII)

Let me circle back, and examine all
This day has seen adroitly accomplished,
To the satisfaction of the distinguished
Archetypes, with their well-approving call.

By this I add to my soul's cohesion:
I've faced up to my failures of the past.
I'll take my earned lashes before the mast,
Bear then, as well as may, my heart's lesion.

Sad am I that time prevents some redress,
For errors committed so long ago.
Some resolutions, then, I must forgo,
And be content with this heart's full confess.

That I do acknowledge those, my mistakes,
Gives credence to the growth that my heart makes.

Rhyme scheme: ABBA CDDC EFFE GG

A Screaming Panic (Sonnet CIII)

I woke screaming in a panic last night,
Distressed by my own failure in the past.
Not being equal to someone's (too) vast
Expectation has caused this great affright.

Someone I worked for, and greatly admired,
Made a request I did not comprehend,
So did what I knew (but couldn't transcend).
In my complacency I became mired.

My sorrow may magnify the problem,
Making more of it than perhaps I should.
Nonetheless, I'd correct it if I could,
Quit wearing this failure like an emblem.

To err is human,[22] so let me forgive
Myself, find joy enough again to live.

Rhyme scheme: ABBA CDDC EFFE GG

---

[22] Alexander Pope, "Essay On Criticism"

Joy of Working
(Sonnet CIV)

Joy of working, creating a body
Of effective esthetic elements,
Finite parts, that function as complements
Which may clever solutions embody.

Striving diligently to meet deadlines,
Their data manipulates and refines,
Is best performed with humble attitude,
To reap our clients quite real gratitude.

When the proper amount of care is spent,
The calculations checked and approved,
Reports can no longer be improved,
Finally submitted to the government.

The satisfaction at task's completion
Leads to self-worth's well-deserved accretion.

Rhyme scheme: ABBA CCDD EFFE GG

Failure's A Risk
(Sonnet CV)

Failure's a risk, in each worthwhile venture,
Which holds non-zero probability.
To accept these terms is maturity,
Living free without Fear's awful censure.

It may be crucial to fail, now and then,
To learn that in time we may recover.
Time, then, may act as both foe and lover,
Leading us to futures we don't yet ken.

And so, the unknown holds some unseen joys.
Courage is willingness to pay full fee,
And patiently accept what destiny
Before us appears, as Time's artful ploys.

If fools rush in, and Fortune favors fools,
Let's be fools, and obtain Fortune's jewels.

Rhyme scheme: ABBA CDDC EFFE GG

I Open Myself
(Sonnet CVI)

I open myself to the whims of Time,
To await fulfillment of all my hopes,
Count Time as my ally (see how one copes!).
Seek from each moment, its essence sublime.

It's Time which I need to prepare myself,
Time to learn to see clearly with the heart,
Discount façades, find the essential part,
Grasp Truth, that most wondrous, elusive sylph.

Thus, allied with invincible vision,
One may tear through reality's illusion,
Bringing to bear deep Love's bright effusion,
To reveal applied spirit's concision.

We are seen now as Love's projection,
In Time's stage-play of interconnection.

Rhyme scheme: ABBA CDDC EFFE GG

GRAPHIS SCRIPTA (SONNET CVII)

Messages inscribed in *Graphis scripta*[23],
Carry secret content, cut in old runes,
By Nature's own hand under ancient moons,
Holding shrouded law (a *lex non scripta*[24]).

I love such twisted musings to ponder,
That Nature should show, to my eyes alone,
Her veiled face, holding my gaze in her own,
Her bright charms, a constant source of wonder.

I am her perfect match in this respect:
I have the gift to witness her beauty,
(and propose fitting praise – poet's duty)
Which others, quite simply, do not detect.

To find in a lichen, blessings written,
Is to be, by Nature's splendor, smitten.

Rhyme scheme: ABBA CDDC EFFE GG

---

[23] A crustose lichen in the family Graphidaceae, whose growth pattern looks like written characters.
[24] Latin: unwritten law

How Would That Appear
(Sonnet CVIII)

How would that appear, to taste of your charms,
Hearing you sing melody, chant mantra,
Your response to touch, engaged in tantra,
Your hair's fragrance, held in my loving arms.

Words of encouragement spoken by me,
To open your heart to divine exchange,
To give our noble souls breath of free range,
Maintain separateness in unity.

Demonstrating the utmost of respect,
For all that you are, and will yet become,
As flower of youth ripens to wisdom.
With spirit imbued, thus, shall we connect.

It is not so much you, I wish to clutch,
As reaching through you, the divine to touch.

Rhyme scheme: ABBA CDDC EFFE GG

WITH SPIRIT IMBUED
(SONNET CIX)

With spirit imbued, that is our real might,
In full cognizance thereof, to reach out
Across the space between, with hands devout –
With thoughtful care such efforts are bedight.

Hold the reins of Passion's fast chargers checked,
Until a proper moment shall present,
When deeper interests it would augment,
Then greater virtues be seen to project.

To serve an unspoken, unwitting need,
To kindle a heart's precious vital flame,
The ascent of which is Love's highest aim:
The growth of others is our spirits' creed.

Toward this great hope my gift I shall give,
That you, my friend, should truly thrive and live.

Rhyme scheme: ABBA CDDC EFFE GG

My Vertigo
(Sonnet CX)

Still I hold, quite still, due to vertigo.
Raising my chin to look up (no don't!)
Brings a wave of nausea, so I won't.
What is happening to this body, oh!

Listening to music, don't want to read.
What relevant questions can I ask here?
Such a strange event, clearly causes fear.
What sound medical guidance must I heed?

It began just last night, with no warning,
No hint that weirdness was about to come,
Odd symptoms to which I soon would succumb.
Wonder how I will feel in the morning?

I think this must be a short-term ailment,
But this moment offers no curtailment.

Rhyme scheme: ABBA CDDC EFFE GG

Whether or Not
(Sonnet CXI)

Whether or not it ever come to pass,
We must act as if perfection will be
Attained and grasped: that all men shall be free.
From this stance our moves shall strength encompass.

Compassion – humanity's greatest gift,
Not logic, rational thought, or skilled craft.
These others are just tools for handicraft,
To build community: people uplift.

To cash in one's chips ere game is ended
Is simply bad policy, not good planning.
To strip folk of hope – discontent fanning.
Clever leaders would seek these hopes blended.

We can overcome blinded division,
But this requires a positive vision.

Rhyme scheme: ABBA CDDC EFFE GG

Love is so Vital
(Sonnet CXII)

Love is so vital, yet sublime. In all
Contexts: self-, interpersonal-, social-;
Each requires attention unique, special.
A full range of talents applies withal.

Insight, to see where help is most needed;
Acuity, to devise fitting plans;
Respect, to accept all races and clans;
Openness, that all voices are heeded.

As above – so below,[25] without and within.
That Nature is divine, is axiom;
All creatures worthy: not mere idiom.
These principles, hold deep guidance therein.

By incremental moves all does unfold.
Evolution pulls from virtue betold.

Rhyme scheme: ABBA CDDC EFFE GG

---

[25] Hermes Trismegistus, *Emerald Tablet*, "Quod est inferius, est sicut quod est superius."

It's None of My Concern
(Sonnet CXIII)

It's none of my concern. Why should I care,
If two women, or men, love each other?
I just care how they treat one another,
That they elevate their partner and share

Their vision of them in greatest regard,
Thus, leading each to their highest promise.
When standing in as Love's own accomplice,
Finally found – a state of grace unmarred.

This I hold sacred, nor any temple
Built the selective, fickle gods to please,
Who, by our actions we cannot appease,
(Though they envy our love, by example).

None may improve on this, don't even try.
Reason cannot reach what Love holds so high.

Rhyme scheme: ABBA CDDC EFFE GG

You Are A Portal
(Sonnet CXIV)

You are a portal to the Great Goddess.
Through shared touch we reach for the divine.
We both ascend, our spirits intertwine.
It is Love holds us, not we who possess.

Is it really "I", that love who you are?
Or rather the eternal masculine
Acting through me honors those feminine
Qualities in you, known well from afar.

You hold the earth's welfare in your firm grasp.
Heaven needs Earth's broad stage to ply its trade,
For without Earth its designs can't be made.
Heaven and Earth, fitted lock unto hasp.

Take all living creatures under your wing,
Nowhere is there any more blessèd thing.

Rhyme scheme: ABBA CDDC EFFE GG

He Who Quips Well
(Sonnet CXV)

He who quips well, is thereby well-equipped
To spread humor where humor is needed,
Slay the dragons of despair – unheeded,
And rescue the moment from Fortune outstripped.

Yet, 'tis best the quipping be of sound cheer,
To deal solemn sorrows a happy blow,
Permitting then finer intents to grow,
That we may forge a future bright and clear.

When nasty vapors vaporize our hopes,
Steal away the instant's desperate charge,
Don't fear! A well-timed quip may Hope enlarge:
Knock those bad-vibe suckers into the ropes!

"Stay that sadness," quoth the quipper, "I say,
With great quippage one may well win the day!"

Rhyme scheme: ABBA CDDC EFFE GG

These Poems I Have Fashioned (Sonnet CXVI)

These poems I have fashioned from my soul,
To touch someone's heart, perhaps bring some joy,
But I'm chagrined when you don't grasp the ploy,
Or project other motives as my goal.

Though I long for connection, I'm no fool,
To have my words twisted or disparaged,
Alter my intents, shan't be encouraged.
I'll keep my own art, not as other's tool.

Unlucky ones, that have no muse of their own,
Or no great skill to answer well that muse,
But must another's special craft abuse,
A pursuit that has taken years to hone.

So, slur not. Upon my art don't encroach.
These well-considered lines bear no reproach.

Rhyme scheme: ABBA CDDC EFFE GG

I Am Vulnerable
(Sonnet CXVII)

I am vulnerable, that love I need.
I am exposed, waiting for hope's resolve,
Wishing with each beauty, love would evolve:
Love built of respect – layered into creed.

Have I missed a consent, there in her eye,
While I plotted high esteem's careful move,
That in the end I did too cautious prove?
In view of what's at stake, don't wonder why.

I need this for my own security:
That she be willing to open her heart,
No, nothing else would ever be as smart:
To know love is real for both her and me.

But if she cannot find her own heart's key,
Then nothing's here that would interest me.

Rhyme scheme: ABBA CDDC EFFE GG

The Salmon of Knowledge
(Sonnet CXVIII)

The Salmon of Knowledge have I tasted,
And sucked the sweet fruits fallen from friendship's tree.
Nature, I find, has done quite well by me.
All those lost forms evolved were not wasted,

But fully-endowed expressions of Life's breath,
Condensed in the cold air of earth-bound space,
Inscribed in the lines of Time's changing face,
Their conjunct *Zeitgeist*[26] squeezed from æther's depth.

That mankind will someday cease is small loss,
For surely something more interesting
Will be born, a new spirit on a new wing.
Our fossils may yet gather shining gloss.

The parade of creatures seen through Time's eye
Should give fitting context to Mankind's try!

Rhyme scheme: ABBA CDDC EFFE GG

---

[26] German: Spirit of the times

IPSE DIXIT
(SONNET CXIX)

Ipse Dixit[27] – Thus Aristotle spake!
And quoth Cicero explaining the Gods,[28]
(Fallacy of logic). What are the odds
Pythagoras did such pronouncements make?

Who may argue 'gainst so learnèd a man,
Assert evidence to counter his claim,
Find just cause to abject falsehood disclaim?
Empiricism says that any can!

Reason is sometimes subject to bias
Of unsound premise, or *non-sequitur*,[29]
Making of truth an illogical blur;
Refrains oft intoned by the impious.

Man may claim truth as his special providence,
But this is not backed by hard evidence.

Rhyme scheme: ABBA CDDC EFFE GG

---

[27] Latin: He himself said it.
[28] Marcus Tullius Cicero, "*De Natura Deorum*"
[29] Latin: It does not follow

I Speak My Heart's Message (Sonnet CXX)

I speak my heart's one true message to thee:
That you are loved beyond your ego's ken.
Harken to what your soul knows quite well then,
As we both search for perfect unity.

Well-prepared this journey to undertake,
We honor our heart's desires at the start,
Knowing full-well with some we must part:
Meet sacrifices to Love we shall make.

If the cost is too dear, dear, let me know.
I will adjust my expectations, love.
This dance should fit us both like hand-to-glove,
Matched step-for-step we'll present a show

That even the haughty Gods will approve.
We shan't fail then their divine hearts to move.

Rhyme scheme: ABBA CDDC EFFE GG

I Saw the Goddess Once Again (Sonnet CXXI)

I saw the Goddess once again last night,
In that trance state where spirits incarnate,
Just before awareness doth evaporate
Into the realm of no-thought: "bliss" styled-right.

She came into view, deliberately
Turned, placed her visage before me squarely.
Wordlessly she smiled affectionately,
Bestowed approval legitimately.

Of course, her presence jolted me awake!
Who would not be moved by such a vision?
Her favor is my dearest provision.
This devotion I will never forsake.

By this, I now don the robes of her priest
'Till such day my spirit shall be released.

Rhyme scheme: ABBA CDDC EFFE GG

With Selfless Acts
(Sonnet CXXII)

With selfless acts she helps people feel good,
Like singing jazz favorites with her dad.
It is these little things that make us all glad
Of the reach and breadth of her womanhood.

She cannot help but attend on others,
As that devotion begins in her heart,
From the root of her soul, it does impart
Compassion for all, as sisters, brothers.

That some may not share such a deep concern,
This thing she cannot fully comprehend,
Her love for nature they can't apprehend:
It is a gift of soul, for Life to yearn.

Of all the things mankind is capable,
Only this great Love is so tenable.

Rhyme scheme: ABBA CDDC EFFE GG

Does Setting Always Promote (Sonnet CXXIII)

Does setting always promote best action,
Where circumstance may lead, should one follow?
No, such response is of deep love hollow:
Consideration breeds satisfaction.

Thought, guided by strong hearts, provides insight
To begin those most well-counseled ventures:
Preparation prefigures adventures.
By this path impetus and care unite.

The dichotomy of a love boundless,
And the uniqueness of separate souls
Vibrates between distinct or equal poles:
We are one-yet-discrete in loops endless.

The tension between these different views
Resolves as altered perception ensues.

Rhyme scheme: ABBA CDDC EFFE GG

It May Well Be
(Sonnet CXXIV)

It may well be, those austere Norns or Fates,
Have measured close the length of each lifespan.
Though that width is a mystery, we can
Still find bliss before death our dreams deflates:
With inspired vision to guide our movement,
Working to promote harmony and peace
For all people, before our breaths shall cease,
So, the quality of all life augment.

Greet outward events from inner stillness,
Not let real-world stress steal our sereneness,
Watch the tidal flows of the world's broad stage
The best vantage for greatest change to gauge,
There to apply our well-conservèd strength,
Making best use of our life's measured length.

Rhyme scheme: ABBACDDC, EEFFGG

Have I Done Well By Thee
(Sonnet CXXV)

Have I done well by thee, my well-loved friend?
I have shared my heart's honest view of thee:
Not faultless of course, but perfect, you see.
On this aspect you may always depend:

I have no agenda hidden from view,
My love is open as any can see.
In that sense then, all is as it should be:
To see my word's effect is all my due.

That they bring you some solace pleases me.
We all have Sisyphean rocks to move.
To have someone notice may Hope improve,
Words of encouragement given freely.

So, with that gift I have done my heart's chore:
To lift another – I ask nothing more.

Rhyme scheme: ABBA CDDC EFFE GG

To Honor Deep Love
(Sonnet CXXVI)

To honor deep love, I've done all I should.
Yet alone I am still, a lonely man.
Nothing's changed since the isolation began,
Little chance to meet someone, if I could.

Can a beauty in the hand ever be,
As lovely as the one you have set free?
For all the time that one has invested,
Has the depth of one's passion attested.

Though today empty-handed I remain,
I have learned of perfect love to create.
Then hope stands that Time shall this skill prorate,
Until a fitting venue shall obtain.

Holding close that hope, I steer by Love's star,
Keeping true to course, no matter how far.

Rhyme scheme: ABBA CCDD EFFE GG

Let the Tide of Life (Sonnet CXXVII)

Let the tide of life wash over Time's shore,
The fossil record shall not capture all
That we are, none of what hope did install,
In the dreams of this grand species afore.

While we walk each day's duty-trodden path
We leave a wake of shining comet dust.
But who will see this tail with stars encrust,
Since none may shield us from Time's certain wrath.

Yet we may stand tall for atime at least,
Through our deeds we have glimpsed heaven's designs,
While Nature's constraints our nature refines,
Leaving a legacy, ere we're released.

Hold tight the hand of God's emissary –
Accept this life as heaven's bursary.

Rhyme scheme: ABBA CDDC EFFE GG

Time, It Seems
(Sonnet CXXVIII)

Time, it seems is a strong love's precious cost.
With this notion I tell my lonely heart,
That refined patience is Love's counterpart:
A truly auspicious love can't be lost.

Here, I have found, force of will counts for naught,
As with casting one's line into the sea,
One's best lure use, yet empty-handed be.
'Tis true all great ventures with risk are fraught.

Experience has shown the longest wait,
Sometimes brings an unexpected result,
Which may even cause one's heart to exult,
So let these minor misgivings abate.

Prepare for the day, with patience contrive,
Until the long-awaited shall arrive.

Rhyme scheme: ABBA CDDC EFFE GG

How Is It Grace and Sorrow Coexist? (Sonnet CXXIX)

How is it grace and sorrow coexist,
When trying moments contain hidden gems?
Events such as these are the stuff of poems:
Glimpses of beauty appear through ache's mist.

A welcome smile, a kind word or gesture,
Can do so much to spirits elevate,
And even help to stresses dissipate:
Deeds tall enough to fill literature.

By these tokens, one may gratefully bear
The challenges, that these times have imposed.
Then those vexing elements be transposed,
From despairs, to more tolerable fare.

Thankful, when angels appear at my need,
But blessed, to see that others share my creed.

Rhyme scheme: ABBA CDDC EFFE GG

UMBELS OF WHITE
(SONNET CXXX)

Umbels of white over lace-fans of green,
Daucus carota[30] – named for Queen Anne.
Pleasant forage for wasps and bees – it can,
Adorning gardens far and near, be seen.

Often noted in Summer's pageantry,
Along with colorful *Rudbeckia*[31]
For companion, and white *Achillea*,[32]
Present a display of floral beauty.

Summer's rain hath all too short a lease[33]
That fairly drenches, yet turns back to steam,
When the Sun from dark clouds un-shields his beam,
To plainly show off the weather's caprice.

I could forfeit the too-abundant heat,
But who would dare to shun these flowers sweet?

Rhyme scheme: ABBA CDDC EFFE GG

---

[30] Botanical name for Queen Anne's Lace
[31] *Rudbeckia*: genus of Black-eyed Susan Sunflowers
[32] *Achillea*: genus of Yarrow plants
[33] Apologies to Shakespeare, Sonnet 18 – revised

Many Are the Solar Orbits (Sonnet CXXXI)

Many are the solar orbits I have seen,
With notable events to frame a life.
With the blessings of good friends, it is rife,
Yet the heart trails after those that have been.
Lately I arrived on the 'mature' scene,
Where Lightning Bugs are the only nightlife.
Simple the joys that one cares to midwife,
Just as are the meals that make my cuisine.

The best fare being that which digests well;
Movable feast implies travel to couch;
Uninterrupted sleep for full-night's spell;
Oft while sitting from wink-into-nod slouch;
What more joys will come, only time will tell.
For these and other delights, I will vouch.

Rhyme scheme: ABBA ABBA CDCDCD

Ancient Tongues
(Sonnet CXXXII)

When I close my eyes people talk to me
In ancient tongues I cannot comprehend.
Though a sense of their words does not ascend,
I hear the tone of their voice quite clearly.

One loudly proclaims the truths he has learned.
I would dearly love to share his wisdom,
From life in some long-fallen kingdom.
What pearls he would grant to me, yet unearned?

What should he declare across these vast ages,
I would know. I need an interpreter,
To understand this wisdom-transmitter,
Who has knowledge from the distant mages,

To gain access across chronology
With insights of psychic symbology.

Rhyme scheme: ABBA CDDC EFFE GG

EROS IS RELATEDNESS (SONNET CXXXIII)

Jung proposed Eros is relatedness[34]
On a psychic level, not merely sex,
As some have blindly supposed: Love Simplex.
Man as species evolves toward wholeness.

Bringing skills to bear each moment permits.
Then, since our consciousness holds such array,
Profound art is to select that which may
Provide results that harmony befits.

The fine discrimination of Logos
(A feature no other creature may boast),
Is counterbalanced by empathy most.
These twin aspects frame perfect juxtapose.

This aesthetic molds my whole awareness:
Heightened focus with committed humaneness.

Rhyme scheme: ABBA CDDC EFFE GG

---

[34] C. J. Jung, Collected Works, Vol. X (Aion), p. 123

Your Gentle Heart (Sonnet CXXXIV)

My dear, I wish to touch your gentle heart
With my own, let soul kiss soul directly,
So light is transferred between, perfectly:
Emergent when conjoined, not split apart.

Do you feel how much you are loved, my friend?
When souls transcend egos, when selves align,
Then brighter than Night's bright stars will they shine.
Soul shall, by love's virtue, virtue append.

So, shine my love, and bring forth Love's sweet song,
Whose melody may enchant the wild beast,
And change rough discourse to fine friendship's feast.
You have this gift, but wait not overlong.

The power of two hearts joined in series,
Marks so well our remarkable species.

Rhyme scheme: ABBA CDDC EFFE GG

Brother, Speak Now!
(Sonnet CXXXV)

Brother, I open up to you. Speak now!
Let your message be displayed, in these my
Thoughts and words herein inscribed most humbly.
To report faithfully I do avow.

"To you and your friends I send kind greetings.
I sit in trance to reach you, close my eye
In the warm sun, under an open sky,
Offer friendship in this first of meetings.

"I am a priest of the great Earth-Mother.
I spread faith and hope where e'er I travel,
And teach men of her wonders to marvel.
To all wise, thoughtful men I am brother.

"I have seen much of the world, and will share
My wisdom to all who have hearts to care."

Rhyme scheme: ABBA CDDC EFFE GG

My Lobgesang[35] (Sonnet CXXXVI)

Anahita, great goddess of Persia,
I proclaim thee *yazata*[36] – most divine.
You, with words of high praise, I shall enshrine,
And overcome lost ages' inertia.

I shall sweep your temple of Time's ashes,
Call forth maidens to open its caches,
Re-erect your statue, refill your lamps,
Ignite the hearth-fires, drive out the damps.

Time has come to re-install your honor,
Your praise once more in song to declare.
The world begs you: your benefice to share,
To precious hearts act as Love's great donor.

Come back to us, fill the temple with light,
Let the people see your love's wondrous might!

Rhyme scheme: ABBA CCDD EFFE GG

---

[35] German: Song of Praise
[36] Avestan: worthy of worship or veneration

Hallowed Words – Hallowed Halls (Sonnet CXXXVII)

Hallowed words in hallowed halls shares the bard.
Open ears hear best soft-spoken wisdom,
Incantations for love heard too seldom.
Harken well, these spells of most high regard.

As the poet calls us all to invest
Our endeavor for everyone's gain,
Ensure Mankind's providence does not wane,
But shall improve that all may sure attest.

Then give joy, if you have any to spare.
It should not go amiss, to the world's lack.
With any luck you will see it come back:
Return gesture to thank you for your care.

Even through such simple and humble acts,
We may yet have untold, unseen impacts.

Rhyme scheme: ABBA CDDC EFFE GG

Tell Me That You Love Me
(Sonnet CXXXVIII)

Tell me that you love me, love, and I will
Be content to hear your song murmuring,
From somewhere deep in the woods, voice ringing,
Resonating sweet and high, never shrill.

My response: write verse containing therein,
Love and respect bound in most high esteem,
Her radiance noted as if a dream,
That none should find there any fault within.

Capture the word that best his love conveys,
That sets his missive in suitable frame,
Tuned so she alone will hear him proclaim,
Unto her in all gentle means and ways.

Read close the words, accept this open hand,
We could build a love that will Time withstand.

Rhyme scheme: ABBA CDDC EFFE GG

Even If She Does Not Respond (Sonnet CXXXIX)

Even if she does not respond to me,
Yet shall I love her dearly, nonetheless.
Something is contained therein, I confess,
Not governed by mundane aspects, but free

Of mortal constraints. A union sensed with
Non-sensory functions: the mind and heart,
Held in open balance, not kept apart,
Until they resonate. Let's start forthwith

To bring their light back to the surface, where
It may bathe the buds, supply radiance
To light-starved grana stacks, in cosmic dance
While cleansing excess carbon from the air.

This photosynthetic analogy
Mirrors work of hearts joined in synergy.

Rhyme scheme: ABBA CDDC EFFE GG

WHEN NIGHT FALLS
(SONNET CXL)

When night falls my loneliness reappears,
By day its face is well-hidden behind
The momentum of the tasks I must find,
But on repose it may bring me to tears.

I pray to the Goddess that love could be
Full-faceted, thoroughly true at once,
Wholly enfleshed, yet endowed with nuance.
For this I would give the best parts of me.

To give, to serve, in the interest of
Promoting health, growth, and the fulfillment
Of all this existence could complement.
This then, would be the full measure of love.

Growth is gauged by the grief one can subsume:
More strength means more to offer, I presume.

Rhyme scheme: ABBA CDDC EFFE GG

More Strength Means More to Offer (Sonnet CXLI)

More strength means more to offer, I presume,
To focus less on needs, more on service.
To sustain this effort, one must assume,
Nurturing care of the self to practice.

Speaking to myself across the ages,
Beyond the ego-voice, what would I share?
-I am a loving man, heart open, bare,
Whose hopes and dreams sit within these verses.

I write to share my gift to whom may read.
Yet knowing this world makes martyrs of men
That profess love, I'd protect myself. Then
How will we rid the world of hate and greed?

By humble example I hope to show,
We may violence and mistrust forgo.

Rhyme scheme: ABAB CDDC EFFE GG

The Union I Seek
(Sonnet CXLII)

The union I seek must first be seen here,
In the ether-world of my own psyche,
Before a counterpart will appear free,
In the physical plane of light and air.

There must be a marriage of archetypes,
Of anima and self, one that supports
The fullness of each, which wholeness purports
Become tangible features, not mere hypes.

When these facets one another buttress,
When these presumptions are found true and tried,
Primum fecit[37] principles satisfied,
All solutions resolved; I confess:

At that moment I may not need a mate
To remind me of my soul's worth-innate.

Rhyme scheme: ABBA CDDC EFFE GG

---

[37] Latin: First made

Nothing Is Lost
(Sonnet CXLIII)

Nothing is lost. Small acts of charity,
May have consequences as yet unseen.
Do not hesitate, empty your heart clean.
Gifts freely-given have such clarity.

Nothing could be so great as this small thing.
Time shall wash the preponderous away,
The intangible is not lost this way:
Time cannot grip what soars on heaven's wing.

By law of inverse proportion, one sees
Greatest deeds made by the humblest man,
For whom else would give like an artisan?
In truth, there are no finer joys than these.

To console another soul's deep-felt grief,
Is best use of love. This is my belief.

Rhyme scheme: ABBA CDDC EFFE GG

Man-That-I-Am
(Sonnet CXLIV)

Man-that-I-am, let go of gripping fears.
Death is but an old scar upon the mind.
Reach out with the heart, we are not yet blind.
Look for many joys in the coming years.

Serenity's point held in tight focus –
A lens to coalesce random events,
An applied context I think represents
A skill to manage life's crazy circus.

It's not something we find by chance,
But the fruit of a diligent labor:
Like thoughtful gifts given to a neighbor,
Or well-learned steps of a favorite dance.

The path to heaven, lined with silver strands,
Is paved by the skilled craft of our own hands.

Rhyme scheme: ABBA CDDC EFFE GG

You Hold So Much Love
(Sonnet CXLV)

You hold so much love it draws others in,
But they will only meet you directly,
To the limit of their capacity.
Don't let your light be dimmed, for it's no sin

Of theirs, whose hearts have not yet fully bloomed.
They will in time given years, perhaps lives.
It is for this that everyone strives:
To be bearers of love we're being groomed.

To shine so brightly is an act of grace,
None may deny. To sustain this glow,
Ensure that vital soul-fuel will flow,
Accept gifts heart-to-heart, face-to-face.

As Love's bold emissary and herald,
You are precious and beloved of the world.

Rhyme scheme: ABBA CDDC EFFE GG

My Heart's Clear Behest
(Sonnet CXLVI)

I have given at my heart's clear behest.
This was well-done, I am sure, for my part:
'Tis a noble thing to soothe someone's heart,
As many before me could well attest.

Giving was a perfect thing, I believe.
My love-gesture was by her well-received,
She thanked me from her heart: solace achieved.
I'm pleased to have helped her sorrow relieve.

Should she not harken to my loving call,
(A call of honest love), that will be fine.
This is not a fault of hers, or of mine,
She would not be ready just yet, that's all.

That I am alone and all-lonely still,
Is for the Gods to respond, per their will.

Rhyme scheme: ABBA CDDC EFFE GG

A Body's Animation
(Sonnet CXLVII)

A body's animation by spirit –
A wonderful miracle to behold:
Charm and wit reside not in flesh I'm told,
Yet display a character's deep merit.

To learn someone's motivation, seeing
The depth of their compassion, and hence soul,
Leads one to wish their virtues to extol,
To acknowledge such qualities of being.

Framed in this context, a friend has become,
The most beautiful of women I know.
Though she feels the weight of life's grief and woe,
Keeps beauty close to heart, does not succumb.

These personal strengths I admire greatly,
More so, when these gifts are possessed innately.

Rhyme scheme: ABBA CDDC EFFE GG

Across The Ages
(Sonnet CXLVIII)

Speaking to myself across the ages,
Beyond dream-self-by-night, ego-by-day,
Hear well these words, Oh my far-distant self!
As a priest of the Great Goddess herself,
Vibrant messages of hope I convey,
As evidenced by these hand-crafted pages.

Deep thoughtfulness and consideration
Within our soul are firmly embedded,
Along with generosity threaded,
Keen to foster a loving relation.

Though this style holds an inherent beauty
It is subject to specific sorrows:
Isolation thus clouds our tomorrows,
Yet to honor the Self is glad duty.

Rhyme scheme: ABCCBA DEED FGGF

Being A Poet
(Sonnet CXLIX)

Being a poet has its benefits,
And likewise, its drawbacks, he's sure to tell.
Though he can find beauty, describe it well,
He wonders how to come where real love sits.

In solitude he writes his heart-felt verse.
Ah, but love is an exchange of spirit,
Between two souls, where respect is tacit.
Alone, absent exchange, love comes subverse.

Since the dumb speak not, nor sing hymns to love,
Where shall he find like-inspired souls to share
The sweetness of open hearts, full-aware,
And the wealth of friendship to taste thereof?

Isolation – a poet's frequent pain,
Sometimes makes of his life a sad refrain.

Rhyme scheme: ABBA CDDC EFFE GG

Courage
(Sonnet CL)

You have said you do not feel very strong,
Yet you act with remarkable courage.
So please, do not your talents disparage.
I fear that would be unjust, and quite wrong.

You hold the pain of others in your heart,
Never shirking to face difficult tasks,
Doing just what each special moment asks.
Such great caring is what sets you apart.

In this respect you are the world's love-gift.
If only others did care as do you,
Certainly, more harmony would ensue.
This observation is my holy shrift:

That your strength is to give, not to withhold,
And this precious gift is worth more than gold.

Rhyme scheme: ABBA CDDC EFFE GG

I Don't Have to Hold You (Sonnet CLI)

I don't have to hold you to admire you.
Doubt not, I don't discount my deep desire.
Nay, that is still as strong as any fire.
Rather my regard is not bound thereto.

My love encompasses the whole woman,
From the smallest gesture, to the greatest thought,
From tears of sorrow, or joys dearly bought,
Each rise and fall perform as an omen:

Unlocking unknown chambers of my heart,
Where before only four were thought to be.
Thus, I may now share new contents with thee,
New ways for deepening love to impart.

As compassion grows, so too its venues,
That soul, from fullness of spirit renews.

Rhyme scheme: ABBA CDDC EFFE GG

I Grow A Little
(Sonnet CLII)

I grow in spirit a little each day.
My daily poetic compositions,
Born of spiritual meditations,
On my so-journey serve to light the way.

So, I learn to expand my open heart,
Find new ways love and honor to embrace,
Set in motion devotions, full apace,
Make of this practice soul-diviners art.

Surely I may become more than I am,
To let obstacles through best care dissolve,
And all my empty hopes at last absolve,
Codify my thoughts in an epigram.

With a touch of humor, for added spice,
A little color, just to make things nice!

Rhyme scheme: ABBA CDDC EFFE GG

Our Tears Have Smiles (Sonnet CLIII)

When our tears have smiles, then we have achieved
A certain level of enlightenment,
To extract value from predicament,
From defeat, serenity is retrieved.

The contagion of bliss is transmitted,
So that our friends may also it contract
(Or some similar afflictions attract),
That community be benefitted.

Grace is communicable in context.
Sharing this can be the finest of joys,
Thus, we become welcomed-peace's envoys,
If harmony is our only pretext.

Laughter is key to many misfortunes,
When well-meant endeavors it opportunes.

Rhyme scheme: ABBA CDDC EFFE GG

Open Your Eyes
(Sonnet CLIV)

Open your eyes, as your future portends.
You are greater than your mind pretends.
Know of sorrows, this is not how it ends,
For you see, you have many loving friends.

With hopes long lost, we all must make amends,
And find a truth that precious Love defends,
Something to hold to, while Life through Time wends.

Our intention to other's welfare tends,
With caring hands to their charity lends,
Thoughtful words another's broken heart mends.

Do not say that love to divine will bends,
Rather that God's love through open hearts sends.
Through simple acts, grace with harmony blends.
In this way one's name to true love appends.

Rhyme scheme: AAAA AAA AAA AAAA

A Poet's Separation
(Sonnet CLV)

A poet's separation from his friends
And loves – cause for loneliness he oft notes,
Beauty not held – the muse on which he dotes,
Yet desire to another purpose lends.

Incomplete gestalts beg for completion,
Final energy states give impetus
To fill the whole system. Gratuitous
New processes obtain animation.

By analogy sound achievement
Of one goal may well serve to catalyze
Achieving others, their costs subsidize,
Until there be overall fulfillment.

To recap – isolation and desire
Have brought change, like a refiner's fire.

Rhyme scheme: ABBA CDDC EFFE GG

The Tongues of Man
(Sonnet CLVI)

The tongues of man are many, one may note,
Forever changing, carried by the tide
Of all human trade and movement worldwide,
Whether born by sound, or inscribed and wrote.

The beauty of language is nonpareil[38]
For conveying complex ideas and meaning,
Or into nuance of feeling leaning,
To the marvelous art of song propel.

Its spread across time is both mosaic
And symphony. A wonder of nature
Evolved from grunts to high nomenclature,
Seen in words both modern and archaic.

So, answer me this poser if you can,
Was speech created by God or by man?

Rhyme scheme: ABBA CDDC EFFE GG

---

[38] French: without equal

A Whole Man
(Sonnet CLVII)

I'm a whole man, as I wanted to be.
I know well my own weaknesses and strengths,
To see my shadow, I've gone to great lengths,
And learned my real worth to a high degree.

The preponderance of the small[39] – so tagged,
I'm content of my life's works on review.
A broad talent range I chose to pursue.
Of my gifts I have from time-to-time bragged.

Yet my best gift is not for clever skills,
(Though by such arts I have managed to live),
But an ability to love and forgive:
My generous heart affords bigger thrills.

No great fame or fortune have I here wrought,
But the fullness of love have ever sought.

Rhyme scheme: ABBA CDDC EFFE GG

---

[39] I Ching – Hexagram 62 (Hsiao Kuo)

Your Love of Family
(Sonnet CLVIII)

I have this day wondered what I may do,
To enhance your self-love and real regard,
To see that your soul is by stress unmarred,
And your care for good causes applied thereto.

Your love of family transcends mundane,
You bear the brunt when some their duties shirk,
When petty griefs cause one's spirit to irk,
Silly vexations bring each other pain.

Your love for each begs them to reconcile,
Quit creating scenes each other to annoy,
Find reasons their company to enjoy,
While for them all you have reserved a smile.

Your love is the strength that binds the family,
And the precious basis for this homily.

Rhyme scheme: ABBA CDDC EFFE GG

The Fisherman and the Nereid (Sonnet CLIX)

I cast the net, and wait to see what catch
May yet appear within those well-laced threads:
A winsome prize dear enough to turn heads,
Or better still a nearly perfect match.

I pray the Gods it be a nereid,
Whose wet tresses are long, dark, and plaited,
From whom the sense of my words is not hid,
To catch the sound of my voice has waited,

Who hears my call in the depth of her cave:
"Come my sweetest, up to the golden light,
Born to shore on Aphrodite's swift wave,
Upon these tangle-covered rocks alight.

"I shall sing to you, songs of mirth and hope,
Not heard by those who in the dark must grope."

Rhyme scheme: ABBA CDCD EFEF GG

IN THE BLACK OF NIGHT (SONNET CLX)

In the black of night he came, dressed in black,
His voice raised in plaintive pleading, hopeful;
Her response was a warning wail, doleful.
Unfortunate, she offered naught, alack!

Awakened by midnight caterwauling
I stumbled forth to witness this contest.
The one begged a meal, hunger to arrest,
But his very presence caused her yowling.

Though part of me wanted to bring him in,
Give him a home, I knew that she would view
That trespass wicked, her wrath would imbrue,
An unholy unforgivable sin.

Some have said cats are such noble creatures,
Yet such ignoble truths their hearts features.

Rhyme scheme: ABBA CDDC EFFE GG

Mutatio Mutationis Causa
(Sonnet CLXI)

Here's to whatever fortune may befall,
As I respond to deeper wisdom's call,
Adopt Time as my complicit agent,
To form a future both bright and cogent,

Bringing my creative talents to bear,
As I override old habits of thought.
Without true growth any change is for naught:
If no growth, then all is just wear and tear.

This commitment funds progressive ventures,
May offer unintended benefits,
Which aren't alone grasped by our clever wits
(themselves subject to salient censures).

Who would exchange their old lamps for new,[40]
Should beware, or else sad caprices rue.

Rhyme scheme: AABB CDDC EFFE GG

---

[40] Mutatio mutationis causa (Latin: change for the sake of change)

I'll Kiss Your Hand (Sonnet CLXII)

Come my friend, I'll press my lips to your hand,
To draw out your exhaustion with that kiss.
Release your stress and find inside some bliss.
You possess strengths these trials to withstand.

Relax. Breathe. Look for this moment's virtue.
Acknowledge first today's pain, then let it go,
Its terrible grip you may now forgo.
By these movements, faith in yourself renew.

Let my words find just setting in your heart.
Distill them down to their purest essence,
For then they shall reveal Love's quintessence.
When you're ready this gift I will impart.

See my friend, how beloved by God you are:
As lovely as the morning's rising star!

Rhyme scheme: ABBA CDDC EFFE GG

My Loveliest Art
(Sonnet CLXIII)

I am creating my loveliest art,
Alas, it may be for posterity,
Or could yet fall into obscurity,
If I can't this isolation outsmart.

Though I feel that some is quite notable,
Accolades may come after I depart,
When times call for poets to love impart.
Then my verse may be judged more capable.

I hope someone, somewhere, may benefit
From love's clear call, hear it with their heart-whole,
Let it resonate long throughout their soul,
Till it raise a spirit most exquisite.

For the chance to enrich another's life,
Pays down the effort of my word-craft strife.

Rhyme scheme: ABBA CDDC EFFE GG

WHAT HAVE YOU FOUND (SONNET CLXIV)

What have you found this day to sustain you?
What little thing inspires the heart to smile?
Which tokens do you consider worthwhile?
Which of life's joys give endorsement thereto?

The morning wren's joyous outburst of song?
Dogs playing fetch, (tug-of-war at the end)?
A hand-written note from a distant friend?
Summer showers that drench, but don't last long?
A portrait-painter's long-labored art?
A flower girl with petals bestrewing?
A young kitten's barely heard mewing?
A loving call from your dearest sweetheart?

There is magic in all these things, we know,
To fill the breast with song, the eyes to glow!

Rhyme scheme: ABBA CDDC EFFE GG

I Love You Exactly
(Sonnet CLXV)

I love you, exactly as I would be:
From multiple directions, all at once,
The full breadth of love, a total response.
Yes, I would be loved just that intensely.

But oh, my love, will you accept this dare?
With my verse, love, to you I do beckon,
To build love beyond mere mortal reckon,
Create a love that is beyond compare.

To love much more that one's voice and visage:
Their very soul within their dreams ensconced.
A love this rich would be greatly nuanced,
Love Magnificent, we could envisage.

Armed with a pen, and an eager heart,
I stand here at your call, ready to start.

Rhyme scheme: ABBA CDDC EFFE GG

Autumn's Solidago
(Sonnet CLXVI)

The *Solidago*[41] not quite in full bloom,
In arching inflorescence, though still green,
Hints of yellow already may be seen:
Nature's bounty evident in this plume.
All summer is prep for this show to groom.
I am anxious to see the Harvest Queen
Present her fine array to senses keen,
Rose her perfume, colored leaves her costume.

Come my Queen! Long I've endured summer's heat,
Just for the moment, at last, you will shine.
Bring forth the melon-musk and the wine,
In suspense thereof my heart skips a beat.

Ah, how blessèd is Autumn's potpourri,
I raise my cup to honor her glory!

Rhyme scheme: ABBAABBA CDDC EE

---

[41] *Solidago*, genus of Goldenrod plants

Life is Accommodating (Sonnet CLXVII)

Life is so accommodating at times,
In fulfilling our need for tragedy,
To bring sweet sorrows, in silent mimes,
Moments of saccharin bliss to defy.

For who should believe the empty promise,
Of love-requited that never appears?
Where is the colloquy that one reveres,
The fruitful exchange that supports our hearts' premise?

For without Love's hope-sustaining income,
Today's venture holds but interest lost.
We should all dread that life's high-mortgaged cost!
Forfeit our dreams, and what would we become?

Thanks, but I will keep mine whole and intact.
A life's contract should never Love redact.

Rhyme scheme: ABAB CDDC EFFE GG

Linnaeus' Joke
(Sonnet CLXVIII)

Ambrosia[42], certain late summer's rake,
Set to broadcast copious dander,
To nasal distress of each bystander.
For who would bear these whims to pander,
When we must endure severe sinus ache,
Which will many a night keep us awake.
Nay, this pleasure I would as soon forsake,
And will give to this name awful slander.

Linnaeus played us all a cruel joke:
Named for the food of Olympian Gods.
To perpetrate this and similar frauds,
He must have been quite a humorous bloke!

I now await November's first hard frost,
When we shall be rid of this sad accost.

Rhyme scheme: ABBBAAAB CDDC EE

---

[42] *Ambrosia*, genus of Ragweed plants

Chambers of the Heart
(Sonnet CLXIX)

How many chambers hath the human heart?
Per Gray's Anatomy there are but four.
Ah, but I know now I have many more:
One for each love I've borne Eros' dart.

I keep secret space for loves departed,
Antechambers filled with glorious light,
Sincere token of the love imparted:
Perfect symbol by which our love is dight.
For those whom I wish not to be parted,
All my living loves, I keep a flame bright.
For those with whom love is barely started,
I'll create new space when it is right.

How much love may this one man's heart contain?
There's no end in sight. Let me make that plain!

Rhyme scheme: ABBA CDCDCDCD EE

My Heartfelt Call
(Sonnet CLXX)

If you do not answer my heartfelt call
Then nothing is all I may give to thee,
No friendly bearer of love may I be.
I'll not be hurt if my care hits a wall,
But stay! Do not drink sorrow's bitter gall!
These trials will someday pass, wait and see.
Look to the day you will at last be free,
When you may once again walk proud and tall.

I shall be there to acknowledge your strength,
Admit that I always knew it was there.
So please, I know you have some sorrows to bear,
But keep in mind they will resolve at length.

I sustain a radiant sense of you,
Have great faith that it shall someday come true!

Rhyme scheme: ABBAABBA CDDC EE

My Father Laughed
(Sonnet CLXXI)

I heard my father laugh at me last night.
It was only a dream, yet surprised me.
I didn't know he was in proximity,
Paying attention to my dreams outright.

I had focused my thoughts on a friend's need.
He laughed at my clear obsession with her.
Ah, but then he never got *l'Homme du Coeur*![43]
Of anything he does why should I heed?

I struggled with his palpable disdain:
As a child I would be no great athlete,
Since I had no huge desire to compete.
In defense I found a strong inner will,
Developed many a talent and skill,
Though his respect I never did regain.

Rhyme scheme: ABBA CDDC EFFGGE

---

[43] French: the man of heart

Play This One Out
(Sonnet CLXXII)

He said: I know things don't look good from here,
But I think we'll have to play this one out.
What's the worst that can happen? Without a doubt
We could be just where we are: So, nowhere.
Say your piece straight and plain. Don't cast about.
Accept the response, beyond doubt and fear.
Know that nothing's lost, no matter how dear.
To your own voice be thus true and devout.

If you can manage this, then love is paid,
Free and clear, unencumbered by desire,
Or abject disappointments' greedy fire.
To such hopes and dreams I have farewell bade.

There is now for deep love a perfect trace,
Onus is on the Gods to fill that space.

Rhyme scheme: ABBABAAB CDDC EE

Wise Care of the Self
(Sonnet CLXXIII)

Wise care of the self does with grace abound.
You possess for others great empathy,
But bleed too much at their adversity.
Balance profound caring with self-love found.

While I rush forward my thoughts to propound,
What you better need is a helping hand:
Advice is banal in crisis' quicksand.
I withdraw my words; yet my love expound.

Compassion in you is so beautiful,
Giving appears like your natural breath.
I hope in the end it's not also death,
As you negotiate the dutiful.

Cherish the woman that you are, deeply.
Give, but do not squander your gifts cheaply.

Rhyme scheme: ABBA CDDC EE FGGF

Is Life Precious?
(Sonnet CLXXIV)

Is life precious? So, we'd like to believe!
But how do we know this is really true?
What truly makes us stick to it like glue?
What excuse do we offer, for reprieve?

Hamlet said conscience makes us cowards all.[44]
If possession is nine-tenths of the law,
Then survival's a hunger in the craw,
Akin to greed, fortune's dark smoky pall.

So, what is acceptable loss of life?
Our congressmen have no grip of one's worth.
(Of compassionate leaders we have a dearth.)
I would sacrifice <u>them</u> to end this strife.

Hear me, oh ye Gods! Take away those fools!
Let's be rid of these compassionless mules!

Rhyme scheme: ABBA CDDC EFFE GG

---

[44] Shakespeare: Hamlet, Act 3, Sc. 1

As Each Day Turns (Sonnet CLXXV)

As each day turns we face challenges new.
Coddled by the illusion of stasis,
We are unprepared for sudden crisis.
Let's hope we have strength to sorrow subdue.

Our acquaintance with applied-will renew,
That we may surmount hurdles – my thesis,
And give to others with love's emphasis.
In my mind there is no finer virtue.

So, lift your eyes to this day's finest light,
Refresh your spirit in this radiance:
We may rise through love's and hope's alliance
To find resilience with this insight.

My gift to you a soft reminder,
To your own self be gentler and kinder.

Rhyme scheme: ABBAABBA CDDC EE

The Adoration in His Eyes (Sonnet CLXXVI)

The adoration in his eyes plainly
Visible when he looks over at her,
Though he tries not to stare too, too vainly.
From this devotion may one infer
A quixotic obsession? Yes – mainly,
Clearly a monsters-for-windmills transfer:
To dream of love, yet not too profanely!
Of beautiful verse to become auteur,
To touch the heart, and perhaps catch the eye.
In this humble way, to sweeten the day,
Has the poet used well his bye-and-bye,
And with preponderous wit prepped the way
For these and other untold boundless joys,
His to be had, when he humor employs.

Rhyme scheme: ABABABABCDCDEE

Got Angst?
(Sonnet CLXXVII)

Are you having trouble with self-belief?
Anxiety issues, like the rest of us?
Have life's fardels got you down? Hey, don't fuss!
Grab the phone, call Dial-A-Witch for relief!

Got a lazy husband won't lend a hand?
Woman, put down that frying pan! Be cool!
No need to call for that long black hearse,
We've got just the thing to fix that fool,
Motivation is what we understand!
Let us be the ones to recite that curse!

Have a parent that is out of control?
A baby-bunting that slipped off its bough?
Or a woman who just won't say yes?
No sweat! We can fix this, or any mess!
Our highly-skilled ladies are standing by,
For all your ills they've got cures to apply,
To be rid of warts, or send in a troll!
So, what are you waiting for? Call now!

Rhyme scheme: ABBA CDEDCE FGHHIIFG

Leave It Lay
(Sonnet CLXXVIII)

Here I sit armed with my trusted stylus,
To present a noble thought, come what may
To turn around a saddened heart this way,
Bring forth the Great Soul as witness for us.

Tell me your sorrow, I'll lighten your day,
Hold your hand, speak your unsullied beauty.
To see truth beyond the mundane is key:
Timeless perfection not touched by today.

Come my friend, and drop this sad pretense –
See it, acknowledge it, but there's no need
To pick it up, carry it till you bleed,
Or cling to it as a wild-storm defense.

Though we all have issues we must contend,
We mustn't let them our futures portend.

Rhyme scheme: ABBA CDDC EFFE GG

My Heart's Love-Culmination (Sonnet CLXXIX)

Here, Love, is my heart's love-culmination:
You are beautiful beyond all measure.
Truly, in my eyes you are a treasure.
Near you I am filled with adoration.

If ever you find you need an uplift
I shall always offer my best insight,
And do what I can to fill you with light.
Please feel free to accept this heart-born gift.

Time will, no doubt, separate us too soon,
Then we may become ghosts-of-loving-past,
Love's sinuous vapor in æther cast,
Fixed in the heavens 'twixt the stars and moon.

This, my Love, I humbly lay at your feet.
I can walk away now, love is complete.

Rhyme scheme: ABBA CDDC EFFE GG

If You Value Us
(Sonnet CLXXX)

If you value us, those who support you,
Co-workers that buttress your salary,
You could demonstrate that most clearly,
While using safe social conventions too.

Toward safety – a cavalier attitude,
Presents as unhealthy, and even rude.

But if you have any place in your heart,
For regard of gracious social custom,
To such courtesy yourself accustom,
Then you may show it by doing your part.

It is not so much of you that we ask:
There's no need to forfeit your religion,
Nor to enlist with the foreign legion.
Just keep your distance, and wear a damn mask.

Rhyme scheme: ABBA CC DEED FGGF

TO SEE LOVE AND BEAUTY (SONNET CLXXXI)

To see love and beauty for what they are:
Merely opposite sides of the same leaf,
Ever-displayed an intertwined motif.
One's love-object's beautiful, beyond par.

Love's the prime progenitor of beauty,
As it thus trumps any aesthetic sense
And does so without intent or pretense.
So, give over your bound-to-art duty.

Let the heart's compassion flow forth,
And flood your aura with this beauty's grace.
In love, be not afraid to show your face,
And hold this state in your mind's eye henceforth.

If our actions create our destiny,
Then let us select one of harmony.

Rhyme scheme: ABBA CDDC EFFE GG

Held in the Witch's Grip
(Sonnet CLXXXII)

Who wishes to be in the witch's grip?
She will fulfill your need for discomfort,
Prodding you to make your highest effort,
Exacting demands that desires outstrip.

We each have our own internalized guide,
To give dimension to our seed-soul's growth,
To back-fill our needs and ego-dreams both,
While we drift through calendar days a-tide.

To my own I owe a great debt of thanks:
She doesn't permit me to fool myself,
Nor imagine my grandeur, does this elf.
Ah, then that's the end of loving self-pranks!

I'm a man of talents and surprises,
Yet also not more than she apprises.

Rhyme scheme: ABBA CDDC EFFE GG

Term Limits for Marriage
(Sonnet CLXXXIII)

Should marriage be subject to term limits?
A friend has suggested that it should be.
We've all seen love may expire suddenly,
When it no longer provides benefits.

And like so many a social contract,
Abandoned when parties cease to comply –
A leaf abscised when new seasons apply,
Other forces begin to interact.

If we knew in advance this would happen,
How should we prepare? Take steps to prevent,
Or clear paths to painless transit invent?
For me: that which causes the heart to open.

Consider this profound dichotomy:
Marriages require work, yet hearts are free!

Rhyme scheme: ABBA CDDC EFFE GG

Gravel to Your Sand
(Sonnet CLXXXIV)

I am gravel in your stream-sand, – which
May be used to grind breath beneath the stone,
To extract milled nutrient, bread for bone,
Here set your earnest kisses to enrich.

Taste them first with your enveloping mind.
Your skin prickles in anticipation,
Mouth moistened, pupils fixed in dilation,
Sense and thought intricately intertwined.

Add a third element to interweave:
Through conscious intent soul is included.
Complete the weave with threads of soul extruded,
Sum the whole being, all aspects retrieve.

With nothing less than total devotion
Love washes your soul – a cleansing lotion.

Rhyme scheme: ABBA CDDC EFFE GG

Love Expressed in Chemical Engineering Terms (Sonnet CLXXXV)

Hearts are semi-permeable membranes:
Love diffuses along a gradient
Of concentration (most expedient),
Until it equilibrium attains.

Although bidirectional is love's flux,
The overall sum is from high to low.
How should one contrive to enhance the flow?
To lower the resistance is the crux!

It's true we all shine at different times,
We each have our own special radiance.
At the risk of seeming insouciance,
Perhaps from an ice-cold heart love sublimes.

So here is a question on which to think:
Are you, of love, a net source or net sink?

Rhyme scheme: ABBA CDDC EFFE GG

No Sign of Strength (Sonnet CLXXXVI)

If we must judge others (and judge we will!),
Then judge them not for such features as skin
But for attitudes they carry within:
What's been gained if we lack compassion still?

Blatant disregard for others' welfare
Shall be found self-destructive in the end.
Without care, social ills we cannot mend.
What's great if our legacy is despair?

Anger is not a family value.
Mockery of those much less fortunate
Simply is morally inordinate,
So, let's just not go down that avenue.

This then, I will emphasize at great length –
Lack of compassion is no sign of strength!

Rhyme scheme: ABBA CDDC EFFE GG

Ego Laudo Te[45] (Sonnet CLXXXVII)

What name bears he to the nightly shore,
Spoken softly unto the passing wind?
What missing love hath his heart examined,
This same name rendered to the wind before?

Will his eyes ever again find beauty?
Call out her name, True-Man, let the Gods hear!
Set the Great Bell in motion, have no fear!
Let its peels awaken Love's deputy.

Toss over the edge this simple token
From favored love-gifts exchanged long ago,
Shared when both their hearts were aglow,
Recalling wordless troths left unspoken.

Unseen threads of thought through the æther wind
From one heart to another, to souls bind.

Rhyme scheme: ABBA CDDC EFFE GG

---

[45] Latin: I praise thee

Two Halves of Me
(Sonnet CLXXXVIII)

Two halves of me are in a pause of sorts:
One wishes to act, the other to withdraw.
The expense of my *spirit*[46] returns nil,
Nor does it seem to help sustain life-will
When my efforts end up like dogs of straw.
Is it merely his own heart, which he courts?

Is there, then, no sense free of projections,
How are we to see the world in truth? Thus,
Could we *see oursels as ithers see us*?[47]
Know when and where to place our affections,

Skip matches ill-made through lens of desires?
In this illusion-built world, what's to trust?
How are we to parry a false-love's thrust,
Take control and avoid life's petty mires?

Rhyme scheme: ABCCBA DEED FGGF

---

[46] Apologies to W. Shakespeare, Sonnet 129
[47] Robert Burns, "To A Louse, On Seeing One on a Lady's Bonnet at Church"

Claire's Sonnet
(Sonnet CLXXXIX)

The Keepers of the Earth, yes – we are one!
Speak our multidimensional names.
Greet the waking sun in sovereign frames,
Turn our faces, let it shine thereupon.

Co-creators of Divine-Love awoken
Illuminating our darkest unknown,
As we set fire to fears we have outgrown.
Equinox brings Friendship's sign foretoken.

Core-star shines brightest from pure heart center.
Good health abides when thoughtful care doth reign,
Proves the soundness of our well-thought campaign:
By good design this grace we may enter.

An Ocean of Power is here revealed,
When rising love with spirit is congealed.

Rhyme scheme: ABBA CDDC EFFE GG

Ignominious Dreams
(Sonnet CXC)

Ignominious are the poet's dreams,
Or perhaps noble, till they reach defeat.
Yet nothing in pursuit remains as sweet
As the love the poet casts, so it seems.

To create beautiful images to share,
Thereby to decorate life's bidden hours –
Poems crafted with intent: word-flowers,
Enriching still the fairest with the fair.

Poems are ephemeral, though paper
May last many decades. They are show-art.
Once written they are dead, till reader's heart
Brings them life anew, to dance and caper!

Magic then, to him, is the fair reader,
To vivify the whims of this love-pleader!

Rhyme scheme: ABBA CDDC EFFE GG

The Amazing Wonder-Jill
(Sonnet CXCI)

Hear tell of the amazing Wonder-Jill
Who spends all her time on other's welfare –
For many furry creatures she gives care,
Whose cute antics provide her endless thrill.

Takes it upon herself to care for those
Everyone else has long forgotten:
Who else would feed the feral-begotten,
Shelter against the elements propose?

Ah, yet for family she's devoted,
To complete expense of her precious soul.
Her inspiration serves to bind the whole,
Her service has harmony promoted.

How may one so much selfless love express,
And not succumb to daily grief and stress?

Rhyme scheme: ABBA CDDC EFFE GG

Ruth Bader Ginsburg
03/15/1933 – 09/18/2020
(Sonnet CXCII)

Alas, Friday we lost a great icon.
Her legacy: compassion-led justice!
Of law certainly no better practice –
A magistrate of the highest echelon.

An advocate for broad equality,
She argued for women and underserved,
From this defensive stance she never swerved,
Offering opinions with clarity.

Her powerful rhetorical skill showed
Logos in service of moral ethos,
The well-being of all was her telos.[48]
Time may show with her True-Justice bestrode.

Her memory will shine, a beacon of hope,
Until we again see one with her scope.

Rhyme scheme: ABBA CDDC EFFE GG

---

[48] Greek: ultimate goal, end

STOP PROJECTING!
(SONNET CXCIII)

I often hear a clear admonition,
To avoid making psychic projections,
Onto other persons our affections.
But even if that were one's ambition,
How should one bring this thing to fruition?
For after all, the whole world's a collusion
Where each contributes their own illusion:
Earth's the stage for our accord's audition.

These thoughts, though, are not perhaps provable.
Based on an indeterminate model[49]
With our inquiring minds do we coddle,
Embrace the unknown, assumed knowable.

If we don't project, then what will be there
To manifest, should no one interfere?

Rhyme scheme: ABBAACCA DEED FF

---

[49] Schrödinger's Cat Paradox

Seeing Is Believing, Holding Is Knowing (Sonnet CXCIV)

A cavalcade of erstwhile lovers' dreams
Parades before us in high majesty –
Let the fanfare blare! Herald, sound the key!
With pomp and verve this day positively teems.

Bound to them we traverse our tight-held cares,
A frame to view against the daily grind,
To measure the truth of all that we find,
A lens to focus, and cut through the glares.

Note well, dear heart, the impact of our schemes,
The benefit to those whom we may touch,
Stone-by-stone the City of Love, as such
Is built of small acts, till it certain gleams.

These Love-dreams have an intrinsic value,
As our simple lives with grace, they imbue.

Rhyme scheme: ABBA CDDC EFFE GG

Love Was No Misstep (Sonnet CXCV)

If you see me friend, will you hide your eye?
For the price of a smile, will love deepen?
What voice will you share when your lips open?
Will Time's constant advance be our ally?
What hidden futures may one deftly scry?
With open hearts shall love always ripen,
Or do weathered spirits sometimes dampen,
Letting love's interest wither and dry?

Why push love past its natural life-span?
If it's true that nothing lasts forever,
Bury it sweetly, with solemn prayer.
Accord it honor, just as it began.

Oh, my friend, all my gifts are yours to keep.
Love was no misstep, therefore let's not weep.

Rhyme scheme: ABBAABBA CDDC EE

The Poet's Prayer
(Sonnet CXCVI)

The Goddess spoke to me the other night.
As I dozed she said, "I am the Goddess!"
I thought "Dear Goddess, my prayers please bless.
Help me find someone with whom love is right,

Who would gladly welcome my loving touch,
Would benefit from the gifts of my heart,
Holds no hidden agenda-counterpart,
Would promote growth together insomuch.

Goddess grant a union so auspicious,
To elicit acknowledgement and praise,
For the manner each other they upraise,
Build a soul-liaison quite propitious.

What else in life could fill the heart and soul,
Goddess dear, that such a love would extol?"

Rhyme scheme: ABBA CDDC EFFE GG

Loneliness is a Poor Midwife (Sonnet CXCVII)

Hear, ye Gods, this heartfelt supplication:
I seek someone to love with open hearts,
Someone to hold, caress when she needs me,
Someone whose praises I would fervently sing,
Someone oft to flowers and poems bring,
Someone to share those precious moments free,
Before Time with my remaining life departs
And my flesh should don mortification.

Though love may not all tragedy forestall,
Without love there's little reason to be.
What peace may we purchase with this, love's fee?
To stride together beyond friendship's call!

There are myriad reasons to share a life,
Ah, but loneliness is a poor midwife.

Rhyme scheme: ABCDDCBA EFFE GG

These Extraordinary Times (Sonnet CXCVIII)

These extraordinary times, I surmise,
Require that we do not grave sins condone,
Such as racial hate, or president's lies.
Justice demands someone for these atone.

To ply forgiveness, where we can, is wise,
So, a strong accord for peace may be sown,
Need for vengeance may thereby be outgrown
While safer futures for all we devise.

Let us allow our best selves to advise:
Let all mankind's shared traits be seen and known,
Our differences not be overblown.
Strength's shown when the marginal we enfranchise!

Find the humane within humanity,
Hence to build a global society.

Rhyme scheme: ABAB ABBA ABBA CC

Social Forbearance
(Sonnet CXCIX)

I may find no fault, where certain one lies,
Overlook others' knowing well my own,
To let social forbearance set the tone,
Thereby choose harmony to exercise.

To have a deep grasp and understanding
Of someone's foibles quite often leads
To empathy, and strong compassion breeds:
We can afford to be less-demanding.

And so, develop real presence of mind,
When we choose to focus on their virtues,
Not be dissuaded by (our shared) issues,
And perhaps our own magnificence find.

Learning thus to truly love someone else,
Demonstrates Love's most divine impulse.

Rhyme scheme: ABBA CDDC EFFE GG

The Dark Side
(Sonnet CC)

What is the dark side of the human soul?
One sees it every day: wanton greed,
Or ignoring another's certain need.
These fools possess no virtues to extoll,

Who mistake lack of compassion for strength.
Scornful disrespect at one's misfortune,
Displays bald conceit, most inopportune.
So, let's examine our hearts at great length,

Find therein the benefice we can give,
Mold our attitudes for the greater good,
And step-by-step stride towards brotherhood,
Creating space where each may thrive and live.

As we all have shadows enough to tell,
So much have we talents that auger well!

Rhyme scheme: ABBA CDDC EFFE GG

Was Gibran Wrong?
(Sonnet CCI)

Perhaps dear Gibran[50] was in some way wrong,
When he urged reserve in Love's exchange,
For if love goes not amiss, then's not strange
To see it return after decades long.

When given freely with great care and tact,
Not bound with desire's grand expectation -
Of Love's deep power a demonstration
May be seen, in its ultimate impact.

Nowhere on Earth is there anything stronger,
Than simple acts of open charity
Divulged from hearts with grace and clarity:
Sustaining souls for lifetimes, and longer!

Since even the wise cannot see all ends,[51]
Then who can say where Love's effect suspends?

Rhyme scheme: ABBA CDDC EFFE GG

---

[50] Kahlil Gibran, "The Prophet", section on Love
[51] J.R.R. Tolkien, "The Fellowship of the Ring"

Folly's Careless Grinning Mask (Sonnet CCII)

Ah, my love was not given as freely
As I oft pretended unto myself.
Always I hoped my intended, herself
Would turn her sweet love to me, ideally.

A jay drops a nut into a roof's hole,
Cocks his head, ponders why it never fills.
Thus, I ponder that heart no love fulfills
When the benefit of all is my goal.

Does she bear wounds that love alone can't heal?
Must one purge until blood runs clean and clear,
Weep until no more sorrow do we hear?
At what point does love finally come real?

Set aside folly's careless grinning mask,
Leave fantasy, accept the healing task.

Rhyme scheme: ABBA CDDC EFFE GG

Steadfast, He Opens His Heart (Sonnet CCIII)

Once again, steadfast, he opens his heart,
Confides his vision of her intense love –
Acting as a goddess sent from above.
By this soul-sharing he fulfills his part.

Reaches out and lends support where he can,
Reflects a high sense of her vital light,
Which even during dark times shines quite bright.
To bridge grief's great gulf, extends hope's clear span.

So that she may this deep vision access,
Provides context which validates this grace,
Illuminates truth that she may embrace,
Thereby realize strengths she does possess.

He frames this gentle view in structured verse,
To appraise her fine traits: broad and diverse.

Rhyme scheme: ABBA CDDC EFFE GG

Open to Those in Need (Sonnet CCIV)

I choose to open to those in need,
Make an effort to ease another's pain.
The world is not here for just my own gain,
But don't dare to think that my heart doth bleed.

Nay, this is the product of a strong will.
I do this as a matter of logic,
To set aright ills near-pathologic:
Social harmony achieved through goodwill.

Balance benefits many, not the few.
Why would any not wish this to achieve?
Love is real, not a dream of the naïve, -
Vital for society to renew!

Thus, on sound principle is my choice based,
That poor social ledger may be erased.

Rhyme scheme: ABBA CDDC EFFE GG

The Turning Stone Grinds (Sonnet CCV)

As the turning stone grinds our grain to meal.
Just so the wheel of time refines our lives,
As to face each contrary thing one strives,
Smoothing our rough spots by every ordeal.

Focusing to reduce our stray movements,
Through consistent effort to new strengths build,
Until we become quite adept and skilled,
To deliver much needed solacements.

Shared sympathy at just the right moment,
To apply a touch here, or a lift there,
While from putting our own needs first forswear:
Thus, to display an advanced attunement.

Our simple lives become grist for the mill,
—We perform gracious acts through intent and will.

Rhyme scheme: ABBA CDDC EFFE GG

WHEN HEARTS BEAT THE SAME (SONNET CCVI)

What can be achieved when hearts beat the same,
When thoughts of social content harmonize,
If we cease fractions to antagonize,
Let generosity rule instead of blame?

Can we afford to extend open hands,
Offer acceptance in place of clenched fists,
Seek any similitude that exists?
Compassion – that's what real justice demands.

It has been said a wise man plants a tree,
Beneath whose shade he may not live to sit.
This is also true of social benefit:
He that gives so others may live, lives free!

Today's pressing *Zeitgeist*[52] does yet prescribe,
We broaden the size, nature of our "tribe".

Rhyme scheme: ABBA CDDC EFFE GG

---

[52] German: spirit of the times

Justly Honor the Goddess (Sonnet CCVII)

How shall I justly honor the Goddess,
Lay my fitting obeisance at her feet?
Her incarnations wax beauty replete,
Bestowing her gifts Life itself does bless.

I call out the Goddess as she appears,
Don't let her escape unsung, unrevered!
Ever shall I be there to see her cheered,
Her clear voice itself to my heart endears.

Witness love's action at its manifest,
Hear the soft-spoken words told all creatures,
Her vast encouragement lines all features,
Finds wonders to which we all may attest.

Love's incarnation perfectly revealed,
Has to our dearest charity appealed.

Rhyme scheme: ABBA CDDC EFFE GG

Healing Has Its Own Momentum (Sonnet CCVIII)

Leave fantasy, accept the healing task.
Then what form shall that loving challenge take?
From deep strength our most cherished gifts we make,
By nurturing others, in grace we bask.

One may not fill a deep well from above,
Yet rising waters fill it from below.
Likewise, from the deep soul our spirits flow,
Rising up bearing a wave-crest of love.

Healing, I think, has its own momentum,
We may at best enhance nature's process.
Through proper care, one's deepest cares address,
Nurture roots that underlie each symptom.

Since sagacity sends shrewd soothing sleight,
Finesse forwards favorable foresight.

Rhyme scheme: ABBA CDDC EFFE GG

Love, Give Me Your Hand
(Sonnet CCIX)

Love, give me your hand, sit down here awhile,
And tell me of all the things on your mind.
What joys, what sorrows have your life defined?
What inspirations keep your mind agile?

What friends have you, to whom you will lay claim?
What insights have your sorrows dearly bought?
What tears have you shed were yet with joy fraught?
What epiphanies have made you exclaim?

I witness the resplendent arc of your joys,
And the searing ache of your deep sorrows,
All those things which Time upon you bestows:
Those blessèd devices soul's growth employs.

I wish to honor the width and breadth, of
Your life's awesome trajectory, my love!

Rhyme scheme: ABBA CDDC EFFE GG

His Bountiful Heart (Sonnet CCX)

His bountiful heart opened up to her.
She mayn't respond for reasons her own.
So why should he sit there, and love bemoan,
Since he retains a quite rare *Bon Coeur*?[53]

Sweet man, who art so nobly appointed,
Lift your eyes, grasp tight this hard vision:
Your virtue's not marked by this elision,
'Twas vouchsafed and divinely anointed.

Accept these cards just as Fate has them dealt.
Life is a tragedy of lost chances –
Ever it is with Death that Love dances.
We approach our zenith by cares deeply felt.

So, this wee bit of wisdom here employ,
And face now Love's pains with determined joy!

Rhyme scheme: ABBA CDDC EFFE GG

---

[53] French: good heart

Fall Birdwatching
(Sonnet CCXI)

Behold the Fall: what a lovely season!
With such contrast of color, light and sound:
No time presents such rich bounty, I've found.
Nature relaxed in resplendent cohesion.

Fields of drying *Solidago*[54] hide sparrows,
While Bluebirds feast on ripe black *Vitus*[55] fruits,
White-Throats, Buntings, flit on insect pursuits,
Phoebe's darting past, like Nature's arrows.

Come with me, taste the cool autumnal air,
As Summer's green crunches beneath your feet.
Learn to step in time with Autumn's beat –
See how she preserves that which is most fair!

Sending her tiny offspring to migrate,
In distant lands their winter homes locate.

Rhyme scheme: ABBA CDDC EFFE GG

---

[54] *Solidago*, Genus of Goldenrod plants
[55] *Vitus*, Genus of Wild Grape plants

Return to Reverence / The Sonneteer (Sonnet CCXII)

Each day's cycle returns to reverence,
As he sits to scribe his poetic lines,
Reaching for words of love his soul defines,
Searches his heart for the means to commence.

Unclouded by cataracts of spirit,
Tender care augments his simple vision,
Proposing verse of noble provision,
Whose love outstrips its technical merit.

Through daily efforts he does clearly strive,
Inclined is he towards star-struck-gazer,
Armed with dictionary and eraser,
An aesthetic artefact to contrive.

Observe: the poet's deft machinations
Coalesce into concise creations.

Rhyme scheme: ABBA CDDC EFFE GG

The Grand Game Called Love
(Sonnet CCXIII)

What a grand game we play, to wit called Love!
How we marshal great poignant metaphors,
Lay claim to expansive arching ardors,
And hope what we state may hold truth thereof.

See the magnanimity of our dreams!
Most certain it is that none may compete,
For whom else may demonstrate this broad feat?
Alas, if only all was as it seems.

The love-poet, at last, is just a man:
His tidy verse, he did artfully compose,
Has not won the object of his heart-rose.
Well then, perhaps he needs a better plan.

What shall he do, his methods to refine?
To the readers at home: Send a Lifeline!

Rhyme scheme: ABBA CDDC EFFE GG

Dreams Pose the Irrational (Sonnet CCXIV)

An architectural edifice growled!
As I did not know how one should respond,
I turned away from this thing from beyond.
I saw a man who considered, then scowled.

He stood up, turned to face this entity,
In a loud voice proclaimed, "I accept!"
Did he thus some tragedy intercept?
His sacrifice held some solemnity.

Both the danger and its ransom seemed vague –
I could not grasp either's significance.
What was the secret of this contrivance,
This angry intelligent alien plague?

Dreams sometimes posit the irrational,
Which Hope transmutes to inspirational.

Rhyme scheme: ABBA CDDC EFFE GG

No Spirit to Inspire or Ignite (Sonnet CCXV)

"Why should you weep?" she asked him politely,
"Or grieve for those things which you cannot own?"
Nay – he replied, my intrinsic worth's known:
My heart's talent I take not so lightly.

This gift from the gods I treasure greatly,
But understand it comes at heavy cost:
My heart sings of joys it owns innately,
Songs of Love's-hope for days sunny and bright.

Since none come near, none hear my melody.
When no ears can hear, harmony is lost.
Without touch, songs of love are parody:
There's no spirit to inspire or ignite!

Thus, since I may not sing it to my love,
Who hears my heart's song but the angels above?

Rhyme scheme: ABBA CDCE FDFE GG

ON SEEING SEVERAL TRUMP CAMPAIGN
SIGNS IN RURAL AMERICA
(SONNET CCXVI)

Along back-country roads past fields of corn
Tall, dried stalks glowing red in the sunset,
Through open farms of brown, gold, and russet,
Whose tenants can't seem to let love be born,

And politics of hate proudly display,
Spewing their discompassionate slather.
Ignore Jesus' word they would rather,
And so, his loving heart they do betray.

Why is it that good ol' country living,
Breeds small-mindedness and selfish thinking,
Instead of creative social-linking,
Where people learn all the arts of giving?

By acts insular and isolated,
All hopes of brotherhood are violated.

Rhyme scheme: ABBA CDDC EFFE GG

Friendship's Hidden Blessings (Sonnet CCXVII)

I offer you friendship, if it please you
To accept, then we'll exchange precious gifts,
Which shall lead to our souls' welcome sure-shrifts.
Knowing ourselves when no penance is due.

Sharing thoughts, we reach another level
Of comprehension-led compassion,
Baring our souls is the highest fashion
In growth, which each other brings, we revel.

See what bountiful joys friendship affords,
Shared moments wax both simple and sublime:
Nothing's richer in the fullness of time,
As we sip from Love's special reserve hoards.

Who knows what hidden blessings we will find,
Through union that fulfills, yet doesn't bind.

Rhyme scheme: ABBA CDDC EFFE GG

Friendship's Truths
(Sonnet CCXVIII)

Just what truths can friendship afford to share?
When all is known and nothing remains worth hiding,
When all secrets bared that bear confiding,
Then minds and hearts may become full-aware.
How honest with ourselves could we then dare,
Without into negative thoughts sliding,
But with truth-inherent joys abiding,
Finding at last a peace beyond compare.

If I call you friend, there is a challenge
To us both then on honesty's behalf:
Magic's proportional to our response,
Defined by the limits of our exchange.
Will we allow ourselves to cry and laugh,
And express love with finesse and nuance?

Rhyme scheme: ABBAABBA CDECDE

Euterpe's Apotheosis (Sonnet CCXIX)

Sweet Muse[56], for whom my every movement
Is achieved in devoted reverence,
Vouchsafe to me a dram of your essence,
To sustain my all-complete wonderment.

Your beauty breathes life to my very soul.
Its apotheosis has day outshone.
Whether by art, or artifice alone,
Your vast virtues I am bound to extol.

Like Pygmalion at Galatea's feet,
Newly enlivened by Aphrodite,
Whose command contains a daimon[57]-mighty.
Yet am I co-creator of this feat:

Through devout prayer I prepare the stage,
For your appearance on the written page!

Rhyme scheme: ABBA CDDC EFFE GG

---

[56] Euterpe, Greek muse of lyric poetry
[57] Greek: δαιμον: power, fate, guiding spirit

Secrets of Good Craft (Sonnet CCXX)

One day's task-set now complete and finished,
And prep for the next day's has just begun.
So, let's see how well we can make it fun:
When *fait accompli*[58] joy's undiminished.

But is this quite true of all like charges?
Could we convert any mundane to bliss?
How then, pray tell, does one accomplish this,
Keep one's focus while delight enlarges?

What techniques best serve to keep one engaged?
Perhaps background music, or wordless tune,
(Though some will find earplugs more opportune)
Devices to keep momentum assuaged.

Which secrets of good craft oft employed
Ensure the fruits of labor are enjoyed?

Rhyme scheme: ABBA CDDC EFFE GG

---

[58] French: an accomplished fact, a done deal

Soft Now, My Friend
(Sonnet CCXXI)

Soft now, my friend, the wind whispers your name.
I can see your image in my mind's eye.
From afar, I send healing thoughts, thereby
To comfort you, your precious soul acclaim.

When we learn how much spirit we may tame,
Direct unto causes both dear and high,
To fill a heart, or added boost apply,
With artful care propitious grace, we frame.

When these joys have been enumerated,
And all their benefits have been extolled,
Who would their collaboration withhold,
Thus, leaving the public-soul ablated?

Your soul's ascendancy has been foreseen:
Is this not the way it has always been?

Rhyme scheme: ABBA ABBA CDDC EE

Love is Stronger than Time (Sonnet CCXXII)

Alas that flowers so short-lived should be.
As bearers of Love's tenderest portent,
That their span hath such modest extent,
Would prefer that it much longer should be,

To reflect more closely a great depth of ardor.
Love, when it is well-given, is not so brief,
May take decades to compose its motif.
So well-sited is Amor's fine arbor,

Grinding-Time may find little there to clench,
When Love, the stronger of the two is proved,
Since it is by Love the heavens are moved,
Patient-Love shall Time's ravaging thirst quench.

Then, 'tis fitting, a temporal flower
Should symbolize Love's ultimate power.

Rhyme scheme: ABBA CDDC EFFE GG

A Love We All Might Pursue (Sonnet CCXXIII)

A person who gives with their whole heart,
Where no return benefit can accrue,
Demonstrates a love we all might pursue.
I would, such devotion I could impart.

This act of charity is more lovely,
Than any form of beauty I have seen.
Of any fond happiness we might glean,
In my eyes this would be more behovely.

This occupation, caring for others,
Brings to play many talents and features,
To the benefit of those dear creatures
Whom she carefully nurtures and mothers.

While the divine archetype acts through her,
I see attributes which the Gods prefer.

Rhyme scheme: ABBA CDDC EFFE GG

Mae, Where Are You Going?
(Sonnet CCXXIV)

Mae, our little dear, where are you going?
Remain within the Goddess' heart-smile.
We held you for only such a short while.
Why should you now leave without first knowing,
The love that your friends would be bestowing?
Though life may even the strong beguile
Accept this strength (outgrow being fragile),
From a heart that is open and flowing.
With all of our love you should be glowing.
Yes, the whims of life are far too labile,
But permit us a chance to reconcile,
Add your name to our love-list – still growing.

We would love to have you stay with us,
But should you leave, we'll keep a part of you thus.

Rhyme scheme: ABBA ABBA ABBA CC

Enough of Egos
(Sonnet CCXXV)

Haven't we all had enough of egos,
Of petty complaints, when feelings are hurt
From snide remarks, or answers sharp and curt?
These must be our growing pains, I suppose.

Families! You've got to love them, of course,
But sometimes, they try our patience, truly!
As when small things are made great unduly,
Or when "talking things out" may leave one hoarse.

I hope the growth we can achieve thereby,
Is permanent, to avoid repeating,
All of this loud yammering and bleating:
To all of these distresses say goodbye!

It takes a special heart to let it go,
And let our compassion begin to flow.

Rhyme scheme: ABBA CDDC EFFE GG

A Clear Path
(Sonnet CCXXVI)

A clear path at last, I have been given,
Not obstacle-free, yet known compass point.
Along the way I shall True Love anoint,
Pass by those cares with which I have striven.

Of expectations I shall remain free,
Unsullied by ego's oft-petty claims.
For with this sight, I now have other aims.
I shall become all that I hope to be:

A man of heart, open to willing-share,
Looking to ignite truth in other hearts,
Ever-seeking Love's and Faith's counterparts.
Join me in this reverie, if you dare.

When we shall have arrived, where shall we meet?
What 'scape will see us joined; twain yet discreet?

Rhyme scheme: ABBA CDDC EFFE GG

Each Love You Carry
(Sonnet CCXXVII)

I can see, feel, how much this has hurt you.
I don't know why love and death, hand-in-hand,
Frame major life events. Yet firm we must stand
On the side of love. Yes, each day anew.

You've given your whole heart, and once again
Lost it, when death saw fit to intervene.
Though separated in space-time, – hearts clean,
Shall a very deep connection maintain.

Despite your broken heart, within heart-space
A flame for every lost love burns bright.
You are the sacred chalice of pure light,
And this fact not even death can erase.

Each love that you still carry with you, thus,
Enriches heaven's bounty beyond us.

Rhyme scheme: ABBA CDDC EFFE GG

Mankind's Endeavor
(Sonnet CCXXVIII)

In the highlights of mankind's endeavor
We find wonders worth true exaltation.
Are these artefacts its culmination,
The zenith of its art, done quite clever?

When I see these things I am filled with awe.
For nothing else sets mankind so apart,
Unless it be the movements of its heart:
Only this exceeds skills to paint or draw.

Ah, here we find measure in charity,
In hands extended to help another,
– To endear oneself to sister, brother.
No other expression has such clarity.

When, at last, shall we these fine lessons learn?
Else we may cease to broad vistas discern.

Rhyme scheme: ABBA CDDC EFFE GG

No Great Plan
(Sonnet CCXXIX)

My life, as lived, conforms to no great plan.
That it should, would be misapprehension.
Life is nowhere written as convention,
Heterodox – life of the artisan.

I follow the obligate career path,
But indulge in all manner of fine art,
Like writing sonnets of deep love and heart.
Not bad I guess, for a man of strong math.

Throw out your old Left Brain – Right Brain theory.
I admit no real distinction betwixt.
Great art is the product of thought, transfixed
By patience, mixed with extensive query.

Watch as artists pause, ponder, and proceed:
Only the attentive ear will the muse heed.

Rhyme scheme: ABBA CDDC EFFE GG

The Rhythm of the Sea
(Sonnet CCXXX)

The rhythm of the sea hides many lives,
Many forms of consciousness are here tended.
All have credence in the deep, lives blended.
Beneath rolling waves of azure each one strives.

Kiss the green liquid mother to extract
Oxygen, required for life aquatic,
To support life-forms from the exotic,
The fossilized, to the living intact.

Nature supports them all, come large or small,
From the phytoplankton to Great Blue Whale,
Shark, mollusk, anemone, crab, and snail.
Many wondrous forms have answered life's call.

Ah, though the sea with abundant life teems,
At times covertly calm and tranquil seems.

Rhyme scheme: ABBA CDDC EFFE GG

Cool Grey Introspective Days
(Sonnet CCXXXI)

Here again cool grey introspective days
Lead one to consider life's questions-deep.
Shall we all-too-brief joys near to heart keep,
Otherwise let nothing alter our ways?

Or choose another path to softly tread,
One that makes peace with a much greater scope,
That brokers encountered sorrows with hope,
Weaving twixt them as a gossamer thread?

So, let us seek this alternate path,
Then for broader vistas on whole-lives dwell,
Let our growth's momentum create a swell,
Accept all offerings our futures hath.

In this way we shall certainly imbibe
Of life's full-strength draught, and thereto subscribe.

Rhyme scheme: ABBA CDDC EFFE GG

Adversity's Sweet Uses (Sonnet CCXXXII)

If adversity's uses are yet sweet,[59]
What recipe proffers savory meals,
When this condiment with life-blood congeals?
Show me this cookbook ere 'tis time to eat.

If excellent sauce marks well the cook,
Then by this craft we shall such sauces make,
And from old sorrows beautiful breads bake.
Note well, we shall no poor substitutes brook,

To fulfill the recipes from this book,
But shall empty both pantry and cupboard,
Of griefs fine-ground from seasons unnumbered.
What a fine spread we shall make – none forsook.

From deep larders of heartaches overfull,
We shall, in triumph, toothsome repasts pull.

Rhyme scheme: ABBA CDDC EFFE GG

---

[59] Shakespeare, *As You Like It*, Act II, Sc. 1

Sigils Are Portals
(Sonnet CCXXXIII)

Through heartbreak a new space may open up,
Foreign at first, one may not recognize,
New strengths to be gained at a love's demise,
But note you then who's downed this bitter cup.

That taste lingers on the lips left behind,
Visible scars of loves-lost brightly shine,
Yet 'tis precisely aging's telltale sign
Which reveals beauty with sorrows aligned.

Those sigils are portals where grace enters.
So, we become beacons of love and hope,
Showing others how to grief envelope,
Of new horizons become inventors.

Perhaps at last we shall reminded be,
What beauty the wings of death may carry.

Rhyme scheme: ABBA CDDC EFFE GG

Invitation to Friendship
(Sonnet CCXXXIV)

Shall we join, dear one, in open friendship?
I can offer an honest perspective,
Unburdened by agendas-projective;
Free converse from a wise and gentle lip.

I hope you will respond in the selfsame manner,
That you will always speak the truth foremost
So that together we may learn the most
Offered here by life's prevailing tenor.

While it's true two make twain, yet often more:
An emergent consciousness may appear,
That will nurture both, and our hearts endear
Through times-shared, that in time we shall adore.

So, what say you? Will you accept this hand?
Shall we find out what our high gods have planned?

Rhyme scheme: ABBA CDDC EFFE GG

Chestnut
(Sonnet CCXXXV)

A beautiful cat of white and rich-brown.
Though he suffered much, took many a pill,
He was brave enough to enjoy life still.
You know you just can't keep a good cat down.

Blindness, hypertension, and heart failure
Plagued him, to name a few of his issues.
Who would remain so gentle in his shoes?
With patience he extended his tenure.

This cat had the moxie, as many do,
To be his own master, answer to none.
Yet despite all, many affections won.
Known by us possessed of no small virtue.

We wish you well 'Big Guy', in the next life.
May it be one that's filled with much less strife.

Rhyme scheme: ABBA CDDC EFFE GG

Scrumptious Soul
(Sonnet CCXXXVI)

If I made a fine meal from my sweet love,
Something to nurture your deepest soul by,
A scrumptious aromatic fresh-baked pie,
Would you partake sweetly thereof my dove?

Feast on soul's delight, a comforting boon,
A perfect repast for bliss in tough times,
Grace caught as it into æther sublimes.
Heady stuff this love, causes one to swoon.

Yet nothing I know could more perfect be,
Than the giving of love's greatest treasures
'Twixt souls enjoined beyond mortal measures:
What could be stronger than this tandem we?

How does this soul-fare sit with you my love?
Is't fine enough to please our gods above?

Rhyme scheme: ABBA CDDC EFFE GG

Come My Sweet Muse
(Sonnet CCXXXVII)

Come my sweet muse, bring your inspiration!
I will accept this gladly from your hands,
To craft my best, as love's vision demands,
With words sprinkled from imagination.

Together we may create worthy art,
Lyric verse to praise all the gods above,
Elucidate the many forms of love,
Showing then the strengths of a loving heart.

My sight grasps clearly love's full radiance,
Does not miss its long-abiding effect,
Knowing this one thing only is perfect,
Though subject to infinite variance.

What nobler office should my words best serve,
Than the benefits of love to observe?

Rhyme scheme: ABBA CDDC EFFE GG

Amara Animum Aggravat Adversum Corpus[60] (Sonnet CCXXXVIII)

Come my soul-archetypes, this will not do!
Bitter loneliness bears but an ill wind.
Naught fares thus well with sorrow underpinned,
Unhealthy despair is direful taboo.

Shake this grip! Invoke that image of self,
Whose resplendent strengths are quite evident,
Whose passion for life and love is ardent.
Take these bits, hold them tight unto yourself,

Imbed them into your outermost shell,
Where they shall act as bright scales of armor,
Against ill spells act as spirit-charmer,
Then as good fortune's harbinger to knell.

Ye holders of *anima*[61] – bring forth all
Assets, that we may them herewith install.

Rhyme scheme: ABBA CDDC EFFE GG

---

[60] Latin: Bitter spirit aggravates against the body
[61] Latin: Spirit

The Complex Heart (a + b*i*)
(Sonnet CCXXXIX)

I have in my chest a heart most complex:
Chambers counted by imaginary
And real numbers (that in mixed planes vary),
Which may between untold dimensions flex.

Oh, sweet heart of mine, what loves have you known?
Do you carry them still, and hold them true?
Will you divulge of them at least a clue?
Have you by these loves more wise, subtle grown?

What is your absolute value dear heart?
We note it will never be negative,
But is defined to remain positive.
A comforting thought for souls kept apart.

With complex hearts we may functions explore
That've ever been closed to us before.

Rhyme scheme: ABBA CDDC EFFE GG

Too Early to Celebrate, or Bad-President Blues (Sonnet CCXL)

It is too early yet to celebrate,
To claim victory over racist scum
Who beat the selfish tribal-hatred drum,
Until the mad one is made to vacate.

Yet I sobbed tears of relief at the news.
I had been distraught at open displays
Of power-hoarding, which respect betrays.
These four years gave me bad-president blues.

But Hope has now shown us her wings at least,
Though they are not yet stretched out in full flight
In time may reveal democracy's might.
Shall we start to plan the celebration feast?

It may take the courts these votes to confirm,
And our nation's best values to affirm.

Rhyme scheme: ABBA CDDC EFFE GG

The World Awaits
(Sonnet CCXLI)

The world awaits the term of Joe Biden
And his running mate Kamala Harris.
Bells are ringing out as far away as Paris!
Let's hope these responses sustain, widen.

I suspect repercussions may result,
Since the hateful voices fear being silenced,
Who felt that their violence was licensed.
These things may make transition difficult.

Nonetheless reason has thus far prevailed.
Those seeking brotherhood at last spoke out:
More than five million votes stronger their shout!
Response to the selfish: That ship has sailed!

When prejudice becomes institution,
Then 'tis time for prudent revolution.

Rhyme scheme: ABBA CDDC EFFE GG

Soft Are the Knells
(Sonnet CCXLII)

Soft are the knells of the poet's fine heart,
Though beat out with unwavering rhythm
The tune is that of an ancient anthem,
Brought forward in time, complex counterpart
To accompany the Goddess, soon revealed,
Returning now to inspire us to work,
To clean out the shadows where dangers lurk –
Let compassion no longer be concealed.

There! Did you hear? Those voices on the wind!
Her retinue comes, chanting their chorus,
In swift sandaled feet to dance before us,
To tell us of her glory – uncurtained.

The war drums will be silenced, let's hope soon:
Mutual concern will be mankind's boon.

Rhyme scheme: ABBA CDDC EFFE GG

To Love's Advantage
(Sonnet CCXLIII)

He ponders time's use to love's advantage.
But is his object to secure and win,
Taking unto himself rewards therein,
Or rather give voice to the timeless sage?

Ah, there shall he manifest real power,
With loving touch to heal and nurture,
For richer truths remain steadfast searcher.
Thus, in fullness of time let love flower.

What say I to one who has lost love?
Friend, listen! You must be your own true source.
Your soul, I think, has no finer discourse.
Deep within love's well you shall drink thereof.

Harken well to these words, my loving self:
To the deepest love, one must guide oneself.

Rhyme scheme: ABBA CDDC EFFE GG

Though I Sit Alone
(Sonnet CCXLIV)

Though I sit alone, at home with the cat,
I have many friends nearby, through the veil,
Whose presence might be felt, caught on inhale –
A psychic thread at both ends tied thereat.

Do you not hear a friend's voice on a time?
Someone whom you have often missed dearly,
Been quite surprised to hear them so clearly?
To feel their love's light, nothing's more sublime!

Now I'm aware I am not so alone.
With these gracious spirits in attendance,
My own is gratefully in ascendance.
To a few my aura has sometimes shone.

"Beware my son, your halo is slipping!"
So, I oft recall my mother quipping!

Rhyme scheme: ABBA CDDC EFFE GG

Dance as Metaphor for Life
(Sonnet CCXLV)

Two and fro, heel and toe, so swing the girls!
Shall we dance to life's rhythm? Step left, right,
Leap high and bow low, steps to fill the night,
In triplet time, as the music unfurls.

Dance with grace my love, as ever I shall.
Shall we dance on a sunny afternoon?
The piper has been paid, so call the tune!
The Lord of the Dance joins our bacchanal.

See how he spins and jumps and turns *en l'air!*[62]
His fine technique reveals years of training,
Such effortless-appearance sustaining.
Then of course hardly any could compare!

By leaps and bounds we honor and describe,
The meaning of things to which we subscribe.

Rhyme scheme: ABBA CDDC EFFE GG

---

[62] French: in the air (a ballet step for men to show their bravura)

Incredible Soul-Ally
(Sonnet CCXLVI)

Beware of him, who thinks his heart is free,
Hearts only shine within social context.
To claim otherwise is merely pretext,
Covering some hidden agenda, see!

What can I say of my personal strife?
I've waited long for someone to love me,
Not the greeting-card kind of love, but the
"Walk with you into the bowels of life."

Where together we should vistas explore,
Find joy at last for life lessons hard-learned,
Exchange our sorrows for wisdom well-earned,
Grind away griefs to polish Heaven's floor.

No ordinary companion seek I,
But quite an incredible soul-ally!

Rhyme scheme: ABBA CDDC EFFE GG

Show Some Spine
(Sonnet CCXLVII)

Ah, little has changed these several years.
The handful of moments she deigns to share,
Finely dispersed does his interest snare,
Yet offers nil that sustains or endears.

See how his own heart, he puts in arrears,
To set her apart from others beyond compare.
Oh, grab hold this winsome wench if you dare,
But should you fail to catch, dry your own tears.

A woman honored and free is not bound
To carry the burden of your desires.
She must tend well to her own hearth and fires.
Only by chance is mutual love found.

Are you man enough to let her decline?
Be flexible, my self, and show some spine.

Rhyme scheme: ABBA CDDC EFFE GG

The Healing Path
(Sonnet CCXLVIII)

While sitting to get his sonnet started,
To get his composition written down,
She descended the stairs in a light gown,
Noticing that his heart to her darted.

Yes, my thoughts are with you, dearest of dears.
How may I comfort you, coffee perhaps?
He picks up a shawl and her shoulders wraps.
To his vow of compassion, he adheres.

What hopes and cares do you bring out today?
Where shall we turn our attention, my love?
Which things most require addressing thereof,
That may through our loving efforts allay.

So, together we may yet accomplish,
That which few alone may hope to finish.

Rhyme scheme: ABBA CDDC EFFE GG

Soul-Space
(Sonnet CCXLIX)

Soul-space, inhabited by just non-ego,
That "Not-I" of every self, writ large,
Until our grasp thereof we may enlarge,
Sure, greater vistas behold when we go.

What lies beyond these confines self-defined?
If our lives exponentially expand,
Our intents with higher purpose aligned,
What then would super-consciousness command?

I wish the world to see unbound by "me".
Out of whose eyes could I adroitly peer?
To see the world through your eyes, love, how clear!
Ah, but without "me" there'd be no more "we".

Enlightenment would hold no attraction
Without you, a mere abject abstraction.

Rhyme scheme: ABBA CDCD EFFE GG

Sweet vs. Erudite
(Sonnet CCL)

Canst thou at once sweet and erudite be?
An acknowledged leader pays heavy fee,
His bearing remote, he pulls from the deep
His own self-doubted appearance to keep.

Ah, let's drop these pretenses shall we friend?
To such drab façades let us make an end.
Instead, we shall griefs with humor leaven –
Through laughter make messengers of heaven.

We should laugh our way unto eternity,
Break the bonds of hum-drum reality.
I'm ready as ever to do my part,
To speak only truth direct from the heart.

Since only by grace of love do we live,
Then what token will you for true-hearts give?

Rhyme scheme: AABB CCDD EEFF GG

Index to First Lines

Sonnet First Line	Sonnet Number
'Tis a lovely spring day with birds awing	XXXV
"Let me pour thy wine, though my hands tremble" – response to E. B. Browning	XXIII
"Love that endures, from life that disappears!" – response to E. B. Browning	XXVI
"Tell me, what are you hiding in your heart?" – response to W. H. Auden	II
"That beauty should be brought to terms by me" – response to Edna St. Vincent Millay	III
"The expense of spirit in a waste of shame" – response to Shakespeare	LXII
"Why should you weep?" she asked him politely,	CCXV
A beautiful cat of white and rich-brown	CCXXXV
A body's animation by spirit	CXLVII
A cavalcade of erstwhile lovers' dreams	CXCIV
A clear path at last, I have been given	CCXXVI
A father's pride could never be greater	XVI
A person who gives with their whole heart	CCXXIII
A poet's complaint consists of just these	I
A poet's separation from his friends	CLV

Sonnet First Line	Sonnet Number
A simple day, and what does it offer?	XXXII
A task accomplished is a joy in hand	LIV
Ah, another evening home alone. Shall	LXXV
Ah, Beauty! You have ever been my grail!	XXXVII
Ah, little has changed these several years	CCXLVII
Ah, my love was not given as freely	CCII
Alas that flowers so short-lived should be	CCXXII
Alas, Friday we lost a great icon	CXCII
All that I am, all that I hope to be	CI
All's well that ends well! So says Wm Shakespeare	LXXXIX
Along back-country roads, past fields of corn	CCXVI
Ambrosia, certain late summer's rake	CLXVIII
An architectural edifice growled!	CCXIV
Anahita, great goddess of Persia	CXXXVI
Are you having trouble with self-belief?	CLXXVII
Armed with sensitivity, a sharp mind	XVII
As each day turns we face challenges new	CLXXV
As humans we are such social creatures	XXIX
As the turning stone grinds our grain to meal	CCV
Behold the Fall: such a lovely season!	CCXI
Being a poet has its benefits	CXLIX
Beware of him, who thinks his heart is free	CCXLVI
Brother, I open up to you. Speak now!	CXXXV
Call it grace, bliss, or whatever you will	LXXVII
Call me by any name, I shan't answer	LXXXII
Canst thou at once sweet and erudite be?	CCL

Sonnet First Line	Sonnet Number
Come my friend, I'll press my lips to your hand	CLXII
Come my soul-archetypes, this will not do!	CCXXXVIII
Come my sweet muse, bring your inspiration!	CCXXXVII
Come, Love, my heart is open to thee	XLIV
Do not go down, sir, into that wild place	XC
Does setting always promote best action?	CXXIII
Each day's cycle returns to reverence	CCXII
Even if you do not respond to me	CXXXIX
Failure's a risk in each worthwhile venture	CV
From solitude I give to you my words	VI
Frost-white frozen man from another age	LXXXVI
Hallowed words in hallowed halls shares the bard	CXXXVII
Harken well, to the mighty morning wren	XCIV
Have I done well by thee, my well-loved friend?	CXXV
Haven't we all had enough of egos	CCXXV
He ponders time's use to love's advantage	CCXLIII
He said: I know things don't look good from here	CLXXII
He who quips well, is thereby well-equipped	CXV
Hear tell of the amazing Wonder-Jill	CXCI
Hear, ye Gods, this heartfelt supplication	CXCVII
Hearts are semi-permeable membranes	CLXXXV
Her invitation, alas, was hollow	LX
Her words, not constrained by standard mores	LXVI

Sonnet First Line	Sonnet Number
Here again cool grey introspective days	CCXXXI
Here I sit armed with my trusted stylus	CLXXVIII
Here I sit, with my thoughts for company	XCIII
Here, Love, is my heart's love-culmination	CLXXIX
Here's to whatever fortune may befall	CLXI
His beautiful heart opened up to her	CCX
How is it Grace and Sorrow Coexist?	CXXIX
How many chambers hath the human heart?	CLXIX
How shall I justly honor the Goddess?	CCVII
How would that appear, to taste of your charms	CVIII
I am creating my loveliest art	CLXIII
I am gravel in your stream-sand, – which	CLXXXIV
I am not here to take away your heart	XCII
I am vulnerable that love I need	CXVII
I am your heart, come alive yet again	V
I can see, feel, how much this has hurt you	CCXXVII
I cast the net and wait to see what catch	CLIX
I choose to open to those in need	CCIV
I don't have to hold you to admire you.	CLI
I gave my heart to another's keeping	XL
I grow in spirit a little each day	CLII
I had no expectation, and no hope	XLI
I have given at my heart's clear behest	CXLVI
I have in my hand a heart most complex	CCXXXIX
I have lost my best prospect for real love	XXVII
I have this day wondered what I may do	CLVIII

Sonnet First Line	Sonnet Number
I hope to step away and leave behind	XXI
I judge by your quite generous response	LXXI
I love these cool evenings here at home	LXXIV
I love you, exactly as I would be	CLXV
I make a concerted daily effort	LI
I may see no fault, where certain one lies	CXCIX
I offer you friendship, if it please you	CCXVII
I often hear a clear admonition	CXCIII
I open myself to the whims of Time	CVI
I saw her come as a figure of light	XVIII
I saw my father laugh at me last night	CLXXI
I saw the goddess once again last night	CXXI
I send these Beltane wishes your way	XLVI
I speak my heart's message to thee	CXX
I stand here as proxy for Love's god	XXXIII
I woke screaming in a panic last night	CIII
I'm a heavenly mess sometimes, I know	XCVI
I'm a whole man, as I wanted to be	CLVII
If adversity's uses are yet sweet	CCXXXII
If I made a fine meal from my sweet love	CCXXXVI
If we must judge others (and judge we will!)	CLXXXVI
If you do not answer my heartfelt call	CLXX
If you see me friend, will you hide your eye?	CXCV
If you value us, those who support you	CLXXX
Ignominious are the poet's dreams	CXC
In a pinch, you can be sure of one thing	LXXXIII

Sonnet First Line	Sonnet Number
In sonnets my heart's secrets I have shared	LV
In the black of night, he came, dressed in black	CLX
In the erstwhile guise of becoming whole	XXXVIII
In the highlights of mankind's endeavor	CCXXVIII
Ipse Dixit – Thus Aristotle spake!	CXIX
Is life precious? So we'd like to believe!	CLXXIV
It is a quite calm and quiet morning	XV
It is quite clear to all just how painful	XXX
It is too early yet to celebrate	CCXL
It may well be those austere Norns or Fates	CXXIV
It's none of my concern, why should I care	CXIII
Joy of working, creating a body	CIV
Jung proposed Eros is relatedness	CXXXIII
Just what truths can friendship afford to share?	CCXVIII
Leave fantasy, accept the healing task	CCVIII
Let me circle back and examine all	CII
Let the tide of life wash over Time's shore	CXXVII
Let us attend the fate our gods have planned	XXXIV
Life is so accommodating at times	CLXVII
Life: there are no promises made therein	XLII
Lo! We are the stuff of which art is made!	XIX
Lo, we cannot stop time's cruel advance	IV
Love is so vital, yet sublime. In all	CXII
Love, give me your hand, sit down here awhile	CCIX

Sonnet First Line	Sonnet Number
Mae, our little dear, where are you going?	CCXXIV
Man that I am, let go of gripping fears	CXLIV
Many are the solar orbits I have seen	CXXXI
Many have supposed: Fortune favors fools	LXXVIII
May we forward walk in soft harmony	XXIV
Messages inscribed in *Graphis scripta*	CVII
More strength means more to offer I presume	CXLI
Mutual love, earnestly sought by both	X (Corona 3)
My day's highest pleasure is time well-spent	XCI
My dear, I wish to touch your gentle heart	CXXXIV
My house is home to myself and a cat	L
My life, as lived, conforms to no great plan	CCXXIX
My little one meows most fervently	XLVII
No more, my too-generous heart	VIII (Corona 1)
Nothing is lost. Small acts of charity,	CXLIII
Oh, I that am, alas a lonely man	LII
Once again, steadfast, he opens his heart	CCIII
One day's task-set now complete and finished	CCXX
One's very life by her own hand bereft	XXII
Open your eyes, as your future portends	CLIV
Peaceful people protest, proposing peace	XCIX
Perhaps dear Gibran was in some way wrong	CCI
Raise then a glass of joy to your fine lips	LIII
Shall we join, dear one, in open friendship?	CCXXXIV
Should marriage be subject to term limits?	CLXXXIII
Soft are the knells of the poet's fine heart	CCXLII

Sonnet First Line	Sonnet Number
Soft now, my friend, the wind whispers your name	CCXXI
Something tells me I have been here before	XXXI
Soul-space, inhabited just by non-ego	CCXLIX
Speaking to myself across the ages	CXLVIII
Still I hold, quite still, due to vertigo	CX
Sweet Muse, for whom my every movement	CCXIX
Tangible on ineffable depends	LXVIII
Tell me that you love me, love, and I will	CXXXVIII
The adoration in his eyes plainly	CLXXVI
The engineer assembles the data	XCVII
The glorious music of J.S. Bach	LXXXIV
The Goddess sometimes appears in my dreams	LXI
The Goddess spoke to me the other night	CXCVI
The inner landscape has quite changed for me	LXXXV
The Keepers of the Earth, yes – we are one!	CLXXXIX
The moment began with fervent intent	VII
The morning cup that pleases the senses	LVII
The rhythm of the sea hides many lives	CCXXX
The Salmon of Knowledge I have tasted	CXVIII
The Solidago not quite in full bloom	CLXVI
The storm this morning keeps coming right back	XLVIII
The time I have spent my doggerel lines	LXIV
The time I spend in poet's reverie	LXVII
The tongues of man are many, one may note	CLVI

Sonnet First Line	Sonnet Number
The union I seek must first be seen here	CXLII
The voice of the poetess spoke dark words	LXIII
The world awaits the terms of Joe Biden	CCXLI
There are two men in my one body	XX
These are indeed hard times throughout the land	LXXIX
These extraordinary times, I surmise	CXCVIII
These poems I have fashioned from my soul	CXVI
This moment holds the seed of all we are	XCVIII
Though a man of heart, yet am I sinking	LIX
Though I sit alone, at home with the cat	CCXLIV
Through heartbreak a new space may open up	CCXXXIII
Through media of many diverse kinds	LXXVI
Time is not Love's Fool: Love's folly wastes Time	LXXXVIII
Time will tell how well I have loved myself	XIII (Corona 6)
Time, it seems is a strong love's precious cost	CXXVIII
To contend with wounds that have been laid bare	XXXIX
To elevate Love to prominent place	IX (Corona 2)
To honor deep love, I've done all I should	CXXVI
To please the Piper at the Gates of Dawn	C
To see love and beauty for what they are	CLXXXI
Today we lost our HR Manager	LXXX
Too wet we are, when so much rain descends	LXV
Treasure these last few days of pure freedom	LXX
Two and fro, heel and toe, so swing the girls!	CCXLV

Sonnet First Line	Sonnet Number
Two halves of me are in a pause of sorts	CLXXXVIII
Umbels of white over lace-fans of green	CXXX
Visions come to me in dreams, which require	XXV
We are measured against the flow of time	XCV
We are poised: Let Time fulfill Love's design	XI (Corona 4)
We cannot fail to achieve parity	XII (Corona 5)
We find at times, indeed, we have enough	XXXVI
Well, I have just survived my first day back	LXXIII
What a grand game we play, to wit called Love!	CCXIII
What a year this is, full of surprises	XLIX
What can be achieved when hearts beat the same	CCVI
What have you found this day to sustain you?	CLXIV
What is the dark side of the human soul?	CC
What is the value of me without you?	XXVIII
What name bears he to the nightly shore	CLXXXVII
When at last I achieved enlightenment	LVI
When at last I shall again see your face	LVIII
When at last shall I achieve this: Love's Dream?	XIV (Corona 7)
When I close my eyes people talk to me	CXXXII
When I shall have landed on long-sought shores	LXXII
When night falls my loneliness reappears	CXL
When our tears have smiles, then we have achieved	CLIII

Sonnet First Line	Sonnet Number
Where is lasting peace found, but in my hand?	LXXXI
Whether or not it ever come to pass	CXI
While sitting to get his sonnet started	CCXLVIII
Who wants to be held in the witch's grip?	CLXXXII
Wise care of the self does with grace abound	CLXXIII
With doubtful anticipation I dress	LXIX
With selfless acts she helps people feel good	CXXII
With spirit imbued, that is our real might	CIX
Worthy of love a woman wished to be	XLIII
You are a portal to the Great Goddess	CXIV
You have said you do not feel very strong	CL
You hold so much love it draws others in	CXLV
You sent your heart to me in a sealed box	LXXXVII
You tell me that you truly like yourself	XLV

About the Author

Mr. Washburn has a long history with the arts and science, and finds fulfillment engaging in both arenas. His balanced analytic/aesthetic sensibility is evidenced by his experience as both an environmental engineer and a classical ballet dancer. As a life-long learner, he is fond of exploring the realms of form and function. He finds expression in figurative art, portraiture, calligraphy, poetry, woodworking, field botany, and birdwatching. Having grown up in California, the redwoods and ocean are firmly ensconced in his heart. A proud father and grandfather, he currently resides in Cincinnati with his cat.

www.ingramcontent.com/pod-product-compliance
Lightning Source LLC
Chambersburg PA
CBHW021955271224
19559CB00028B/395